]
ꭓ   now
t   r at
                                                                       esan
Children's Committee. An accredited Godly Play teacher, her
MA (Pastoral Theology) dissertation explored storytelling in
relation to children's spirituality.

Dedicated to Claire and James, whose questions many years ago started me thinking about their understanding of God

UNDERSTANDING CHILDREN UNDERSTANDING GOD

Ronni Lamont

First published in Great Britain in 2007

Society for Promoting Christian Knowledge
36 Causton Street
London SW1P 4ST

British Library Cataloguing-in-Publication Data
A catalogue record for this book is available from the British Library

ISBN 978–0–281–05820–4

1 3 5 7 9 10 8 6 4 2

Typeset by Graphicraft Ltd, Hong Kong
Printed in Great Britain by Ashford Colour Press

Produced on paper from sustainable forests

Contents

Acknowledgements

———◆◆◆———

Thanks to the staff and children of Old Bexley (Church of England) Primary School and Hurst Primary School for their hospitality and sharing of themselves,

to George Dewhurst and Raylia Chadwick and others for relaying stories of children's faith to me,

to my husband, Gordon, for encouragement and the IT skills that saved my manuscript,

and to the people of St John the Evangelist in Bexley who let me take the time to write.

Ronni Lamont <www.creativespirituality.org.uk>

Introduction

It was my week to tell the story in Sunday school. I told the story, we sang some songs and said a prayer, and I went into church, to do my bit for the rest of the congregation. Later on, Sophie (aged 6) came up to me;

'Ronni, you've got very big black boots.'

'Yes, Sophie, that's because I've got big feet.'

'God must have enormous boots, Ronni.'

I think I replied something like: 'Yes, God must have enormous boots, mustn't he, Sophie . . .'

Children say things that adults do not. It's partly social conditioning, partly self-consciousness and not wanting to look foolish, but it's also because children think differently from adults. St Paul was right when he said

> When I was a child, I spoke like a child, I thought like a child, I reasoned like a child; when I became an adult, I put an end to childish ways.[1]

As children grow up, their thinking processes change, so they stop thinking childish thoughts.[2] The premise of this book is that we should value what children say in their childish way, as it opens back up to adults the child's rightly childish view of God. Deep within us all is the child who thought in childish ways and spoke in childish ways: the way of thinking, speaking and being before self-consciousness strikes, and we become tongue-tied and less able to share our innate spirituality.

Without listening to our children we cannot recapture that very different way of doing theology, which many in our

vii

culture perceive as somehow 'less' than an adult way of doing theology.

Jerome Berryman, in his introductory book entitled *Godly Play*,[3] states his clearly held belief that children are born with knowledge of God, and that this is as natural to them as breathing. It is as we grow up that we lose that innate belief, as we ask the inevitable questions of our childish belief and take on the values of the largely secular world around us. Our awareness of the world overpowers this spirituality, and we lose that knowledge of God with us, even if we did not have the name for God.

Jesus told us that unless we become as children, we cannot enter the kingdom of heaven. There have been many interpretations of that radical statement. This book explores a child's spirituality and view of God and the kingdom of heaven, hoping that by understanding children, we adults will be helped to understand God.

The first chapters of the book give an overview of the psychological theories that have been developing over the last 100 years, tools to help us understand the children that we work with. Please don't be tempted to skip over these chapters – they are critical if we are to understand where Sophie's comment came from. These tools help us to re-enter that place where we have once been and now find it so hard to return to – the place where God is so present for many of our children.

The later chapters of the book contain some practical ideas and strategies on how, I believe, we can work with and learn from our children as we journey together in our lives of faith.

1

What is spirituality?

<hr>

God means Good to me. And my family. The best thing is God.
When I am lonely I think of God and I feel better.

(Marayyam, 8)

What do I mean when I use the word 'spirituality'? What do
you mean when you use the word? 'Spirituality' is a vague
word, one that is commonly heard, but not often in the same
sentence as 'church', 'worship', 'congregation', 'Sunday school'.
Today's concept of spirituality is exceptionally slippery, and very
subjective to the person using the word. I have a friend who
describes herself as 'spiritual but not religious' and therein
may lie the nub of the matter.

My computer thesaurus defines 'spirituality' as: 'religion,
theology, religious studies, mysticism, holiness'.

The aim of this chapter is to examine what the word 'spirituality' means to me, and therefore to help you to examine
what it means for you. We will then move on to looking at what
it might mean within the confines of this book.

A good way into this discussion is through my friend's comment above. She is spiritual but not religious. Thirty years ago
she was also religious, but now she worships with the Friends
(Quakers) and does not describe herself as a religious person.
What does this mean? Many people would agree, describing
themselves as spiritual but on the agnostic or atheistic end of
the 'belief in God' spectrum.

Try this for yourself. Ask people what they think the word 'spirituality' means. They will probably reply using words such as 'love', 'peace', 'inner self', 'hope', 'tranquillity'. They may mention religious belief, as my thesaurus did, but if they live outside organized religion, it will come later in their personal list.

Now ask them what 'religion' means. They'll probably use words such as 'church', 'funeral', 'marriages', 'baptism', 'Christmas', 'Easter', 'Christians', 'Moslems', etc. The two lists do not have all that many words in common, and the tone of the two lists is different; the list to do with 'spirituality' feels more positive, more desirable in this day and age. 'Religion' comes across as a more negative concept, more to do with 'Thou shalt not' than 'Thou shalt'. One is very personal, the second much more to do with society and our institutions. One is full of the desirables of a full and inclusive, holistically healthy life, the other of optional add-ons for those who require such things. Religion can sometimes cause as many problems as it gives answers. Spirituality is thought of as an opening up, a third dimension to life, and one that most people are very positive about. Religion – well, that depends on what this week's headlines are as to how positively people respond to the word and all the baggage it brings with it. Religion is now thought of by many in the population as controlling and unhelpful, while spirituality is liberating and seen to be advantageous in one's personal inner journey.

In the book *The Spirit of the Child*,[4] the relationship between spirituality and religion is modelled as a tree, where the roots are a person's spirituality and the leaves are her religion. Thus the spirituality is the deep-down, unseen part of the person's faith life, and the leaves, so conspicuous and clear, mark her out as religious. The metaphor could be taken to extremes – perhaps Anglicans are oak trees, Roman Catholics sycamores, Moslems . . . and the last comment to make before the metaphor is taken to ridiculous extremes is that while the leaves may

2

indeed fall off a tree, it's only dead when the roots die. So it is that people may well be spiritual without any trappings of religious belief or conviction. These people may only go to church or a place of worship to mark the important rites of passage for their family or others, such as weddings or funerals. They may be among the millions who regularly attend at Christmas and Easter, but not usually in between. They may be among the millions who went regularly as children, but stopped when something else became more important on a Sunday. Or they may be among the many people who like to enter churches when they are empty, to think and commune with their inner being without any overt guidance as to how that process should be undertaken. I would encourage all who are reading this book to notice the spirituality that flows through all human beings, or at least has the potential to be there within each of us. And this applies to children especially.

This common potential spirituality was brought to notice for our age in particular through the work of Alister Hardy, who, as retired Chair of Zoology at Oxford University, gave the Gifford Lectures at Aberdeen in 1965. In these lectures, Hardy, a committed Darwinist, stated that he believed that religious experience has evolved through the process of natural selection, and that being religious in some way gave *Homo sapiens* an evolutionary edge. Having religious belief was of survival value to the individual. He was saying that there is a form of awareness that is over and above our 'normal' awareness of what is going on around us, and which transcends that everyday awareness. This special awareness is potentially present in all human beings and has a positive function in our lives, enabling us to survive, and the many religions that are present in our world are the natural outworkings of that transcendent awareness. The religions of the world vary according to the culture in which they arise, taking local cultural norms and refining the religion to reflect and reinforce those particular norms. Hardy also believed that religious awareness is an expression of a physical predisposition or a process that is present for all of us, and that there is a section of the brain that has evolved to undertake this awareness. The awareness is not 'owned' by any one religion, but those religions show that it is indeed common right across the globe, in all cultures. It is even seen in people who are alienated from religious culture, and this may be an increasingly important observation in our increasingly secular society. Thus this religious awareness is thought to be potentially present in all of us.

There are various theories as to how this spiritual awareness became the religions that we now see around us in the world. Religion may come from ancient philosophies, with traditional philosophy underpinning the particular form of faith. Or it may be that it is an outworking of a common experience, a spiritual awareness that is common to humanity. Or, again, it could be that that religious experience is coming out of a culture, and entering a religion means that you have to become competent in the language of that particular religion. It could be a combination of these three theories, but the last means that if anyone is to comprehend and grow in their chosen religion, it is imperative that they have the language to negotiate that faith. How could anyone be a Christian without hearing the word 'sin' and understanding what that tiny but powerful word means?[5] Yet we assume that when we say 'sin', everyone listening knows what that means. The same is true for all the language that is used within the context of the Church and its workings. Religious language is a clear form of jargon (a specific set of words and concepts necessary to an area of understanding), and if we do not ensure that those who are joining our faith are clearly helped to understand its vocabulary, they will not be able to access worship or anything more than a very basic form of teaching. This is an important idea, and one that we will return to later.

So, across the globe, this awareness gave rise to religions. It is this awareness that many people define as 'spirituality'.

Since the lectures, the Alister Hardy Institute (first at Oxford and now at Lampeter University), followed by the Spirituality Research at Nottingham University, among others, has published work investigating the common spiritual experiences of human beings in the UK. Approximately 50 per cent of the population will acknowledge having had such an experience, many in childhood, many when the person was alone. The experiences are often spoken about as sensing a presence, and of the person knowing that the presence was good and loving. In a recent conversation, I heard the story of how, after giving birth, a woman was left on her own, and she saw a beautiful blue-white light in the room. She knew that this was God, and that great goodness was emanating from the light. To this day, she still puzzles over the 'why?'

It is worth noting that people who are not able to access a good quality of life, who are oppressed and unable to articulate well, will be less likely to speak of a religious experience, and that there is a significant association between having a spiritually rich inner life with good health and personal happiness.[6]

There are suggestions in the research that spirituality is more evidently present in children than in adults. This may be due to the pattern of western culture, where there is an expectation that we keep our religious experiences to ourselves (but in my experience, if you do speak of your spiritual life it's like taking a cork out of a bottle) and so our spirituality is an internal affair, little discussed and not related to the mainstream consciousness around us. As children grow up, they recognize that adults don't speak of or share their spiritual lives, and so neither will the children. Sadly, this means that many adults don't even have the language needed to share their spiritual lives, should they wish so to do.[7] One of our tasks as teachers is to give children and adults the language with which they can articulate and explore their spiritual lives, be they inside or outside of a religious context.

Children and spirituality

Heaven lies about us in our infancy!
Shades of the prison-house begin to close
  Upon the growing Boy,
But he beholds the light, and whence it flows,
  He sees it in his joy;
The Youth, who daily farther from the east
  Must travel, still is nature's Priest
  And by the vision splendid
  Is on his way attended;
At length the Man perceives it die away,
And fade into the light of common day.[8]

There is an apocryphal story about a poet who was a contemporary of Wordsworth: when he came across a woman with a newborn baby, he picked up the baby and sternly asked the child to 'Tell me, tell me what it was like . . .'

Within the above lines there is a profound realization that children have a glimpse of heaven within their souls that is lost as they mature, that they find thinking about spirituality far easier than adults, and that ability to be in touch with themselves at this profound level is lost as they 'mature'.

I once read that the eyes of a newborn child are unfocused as the child's soul hasn't quite arrived yet, and that their look is direct from heaven.[9] This relates to Augustine's theory that we revisit in the prayer 'O God, our hearts are restless until they find their rest in you . . .' referring to his (presently orthodox) belief that all souls are present with God in heaven before they join their human shape, and then return to God in heaven when that human shape has expired.

So what happens to our children's easy spirituality? There is no doubt that, as they grow up, they absorb far more about life from the modelling that they experience from those around them than from their words. So I may tell my children to share their insights about God and the world, but if I don't share my experiences and ideas with them as easily as they share theirs with me, they are going to notice, very quickly, that this isn't an area of conversation that adults easily enter. What goes on at home, even in an open home where such discussions are welcomed, is not mirrored in life, so the children will hold on to their insights, perhaps sharing them at home or at church, but then, eventually, probably not sharing them at all. As children enter into adolescence, other thoughts and activities crowd in upon them, and peer pressure along with the changes that we discuss later will press out their easy understanding of spirituality. If they don't talk about their spirituality, they won't grow in their use of more sophisticated language to help them to understand increasingly sophisticated spiritual–religious concepts, and so their reasoning stalls and stops.

It is clear that the way forward is to listen to what children have to say, to listen attentively and so draw alongside them, imagining as much of their inner life as we can, and then go there to help them. This is, of course, easier said than done. When my thinking is that of an adult, and theirs is that of a child (see Chapter 2 on cognitive development for a clearer understanding of the difference) this can feel like running up a slope, but it is what we need to do. And, like running up that slope, it gets easier with practice.

Children's spiritual awareness is revealed in many ways.[10] First, they are very aware; they can 'feel' a mood and are easily taken there by music or by looking at pictures. Light a candle and let a child hold it, and watch the rapture on his face as he looks into the flame. Like many clergy, I resisted Christingle services on grounds of 'health and safety', but I now have the service because an adult told me how much it meant to her as a child – it was one of her key moments in her growth in faith as a Christian.

Children can focus in on the mood and dwell in the moment far better than most adults. This is partly because, unlike me, they're not wondering what to cook for supper, or where that top came from that someone's wearing, or whether I primed the alarm as I left the house . . . If we can leave all our external fretting behind, we too can enter into the magic of the child's concentration on a simple candle flame, a flock of birds, a newborn lamb or even a plane taking off.

Children will be excited by many things that adults ignore simply because we're so used to them, and if we can go there with them our world will open up and become the sparkling place that children occupy in these moments.

This period of a child's life is not eternal – at the point where language and symbols begin to merge in the mind, children lose the ability to just 'be' as they try to behave in a more 'adult' manner. Enjoy it while you can!

Because children are sensitive and are easily taken into a mood, we need to ensure we are not manipulating them to a place where we can push them towards something that they may otherwise not agree to. I have been at events where children are urged to respond to an altar call to commit their lives to Christ; while it may seem very successful, the children are more likely to have been responding to the adult (probably unconsciously) manipulating the mood of the event, and from children's love of being in with the others and following the crowd. In my opinion, such an altar call is not appropriate for children.

Children have a great sense of awe. They will stop at the brow of a hill and just look, taking in the vista. When the children from the local school come to look round my church, the ones who have never been in before often stop in the doorway with their jaws open. 'What an enormous place, so high, so beautiful,' they seem to be thinking. The building itself was of course designed by the Victorians to inspire awe, and it is achieving that aim in these children. I remember as a child going to (a modern) church for choir practice one evening. There were no adults there, so we 'dared' each other to touch the altar table. I was terrified, and quite expected a bolt of lightning to send me on my way. It didn't, but I can still remember the feeling of intruding into a 'holy space' where I felt I had no right to be. Saying the words of the prayer of consecration after being ordained was similar – somehow it's always someone else who does this . . . Recently, while going through a preparation course for our children to receive communion prior to being confirmed (see Chapter 10), we asked the children to go and sit somewhere that they felt was holy, where they could feel close to God. Two shared my seat (in the chancel area, behind a screen). Two went up and sat by the altar. Another sat on the organist's seat, another couple up in the pulpit, others around the chancel, inside the 'holy' area defined by the screen that extends across the church. They had a very clear sense of where the holy part of the church was, and entered that area with some trepidation the first time.

We see children's spirituality through their use of the imagination. Read through some of the comments from children that are included in this book – they are stunningly imaginative about God, and God's life and activity in the world.

I think God is my best friend. He makes me happy when I'm sad and I think of him when I am lonely. When I close my eyes we sing songs to each other. I love it.

(Ruby, 8)

Anyone who works with children will have such examples to give of how children experience God in the imagination as they go through life. For me, it is one of the greatest joys of working with children.

Children understand that God is good, and they understand this in a quite sophisticated way. They seek God when unhappy, expecting God to come close and cheer them up, providing company when lonely and even as someone to sing with!

Many adults will be familiar of the experience of music taking you out of yourself, to a 'higher plane'. This is familiar too for children, who will listen intently to music, clearly 'miles away' in their enjoyment. Similarly, a walk through woods or the local park may give a similar raised awareness in any of us, and children are particularly open to this, watching birds and animals with more patience than many adults.

You may also be familiar with the feeling of not thinking about something that you do well, that is effortless. My best experiences of this have been when dancing, or galloping on a horse that knows exactly at which point to slow down because you're nearing the end of the gallop. This is called 'flow' and is common to most people. Ask them what they were thinking about at that point and they may give you a puzzled look – they were just there, in the moment.

Adults will feel very grateful for these spiritual moments breaking into their lives, while children seem to have a more seamless join between their spiritual and physical experiences.

You may be thinking that I'm now beginning to describe the better religious rituals that you have been to; indeed, the theory is that our worship should take people to a place where they let go of their consciousness and just 'go with the flow'. Thus our awareness of the spiritual is heightened, for adults as well as for children. You may also be thinking that some of the experiences I've described are not what you would usually call 'spiritual'. Perhaps one of the tasks of this book is to encourage religious folk to let the world share a concept that we have for many years felt was our own private affair.

Spirituality is all around us and within us. We have briefly considered how it is integrated into each individual, and in the next few chapters we move on to consider how children develop in various ways, becoming the multifaceted individuals that we all are, and to see where spirituality is to be found in that blend.

Questions for discussion

1 What do you mean by 'spirituality'? Perhaps write up your group's comments on a flip-chart and see if you can reach a common mind or a definition for your place of worship.

2 Do you agree that people can be spiritual without being religious? If not, can you say what is resisting this idea within you?

3 What words found within your worship do you find it difficult to explain to children? Or to adults?

4 Can you remember any religious acts, or services, which you found particularly meaningful? Would you be prepared to share these with the group?

5 What other experiences in life would you now describe as spiritual?

2

Intellectual development

———◆◆◆———

As a curate in 1959 I was taking a class of 5- and 6-year-olds (St Peter's, Chorley, Diocese of Blackburn). The subject was 'Saints', and near the end of the lesson we had a list of 200 saints' names on the blackboard. Then the bell sounded for the mid-morning break. Everyone left except a little girl, Jean. 'What's the matter?' I asked . . . 'We have missed one out,' she said . . . 'Who?' I asked . . . 'St Freddie,' came her reply . . . 'Do you know about St Freddie?' I asked . . . 'Oh yes,' came the reply . . . 'Do tell me,' I said. This was her reply: 'Well, you see, Curate, when I was 4 my mum had a little baby and we called him Freddie, but when he was ten days old . . . he died.' 'Oh, I am sorry,' I interjected . . . 'Oh, it's all right,' she continued, ''cos you see, Curate, if a saint is somebody who never did or said anything wrong to anybody then we have a saint in our family, and his name is Freddie.' We wrote the name St Freddie on the blackboard and off she went, skipping into the playground to join her friends.

(George Dewhurst)

Just how do children's minds develop as they grow older? A baby is so different from a toddler, the toddler so different from a primary aged child, the child so different from an adolescent, the adolescent so different from an adult. This chapter looks at the theories of how this amazing process takes place and how we see intellectual development through the ways and being of a child.

Intellectual development

Broadly speaking, there are three views at the moment held among psychologists about a child's intellectual development. The *psychometric* view is based on measuring a child's intelligence, giving measures such as IQ. However, it does not include the perceptible fact that as children grow older their thinking changes and becomes more abstract. This led to a second view, *cognitive development*, which focuses on structures rather than intellectual power, looking at the way that children are changing the way they handle new information or data, and concentrating on the common traits of thinking that all children display rather than how clever each child is. Today, these two models have been partially integrated to give the *information processing approach* which regards intelligence not as a faculty or trait of the mind, but as about processing.

There is little to say about psychometric theories other than that 11+ type exams are often still based upon them. You can indeed measure a person's IQ, and while that will tell you how intelligent she is, it is a very one-dimensional snapshot of that person at this particular moment. Ironically, it does not discriminate between which subject areas the person is good at. My son at 13 had quite a high IQ, but was only average (by the school's definition) at maths. This was confusing for his new school when we moved house – one overall score doesn't define strengths and weaknesses.

IQ tests continue to be used, but most organizations that test folk will use a more wide-ranging form of psychometric testing. Hopefully we no longer value people just for their IQ, but that's another story.

When I went to teacher training college, many years ago, I learned about the theory of cognitive (intelligence) development, as put forward by Jean Piaget. One of our lecturers, whom we liked to impersonate, had a favourite saying: 'Trying to understand Piaget is like trying to start a car on a cold morning.'

And that tells you that it *was* many years ago! At that time, we were taught Piaget rather as if he was the gospel truth; now there has been time for developments and more research and Piaget is less revered. But there is still value in looking at his theory – much of it will resonate within those of us who have watched children at play or at work.

Jean Piaget (1896–1980) looked at the form and structure of children's thinking as they develop over the years. He asked the question 'How do children understand the world around them?', going on to look at what kind of logic they use to help them comprehend the world in which they live and how that logic changes as they grow older.

He started with 'How does a child's knowledge of the world develop?' making the central assumption that children are active participants in the development of their internal knowledge – that they reach out to the world to learn all about it and so take part in it. He thought that as children grow older, they construct their own understanding of what is happening to them and within them.

This means that everyone thinks differently, and that is so important for us all to take on board. Every single person's brain works differently, and children are very different from adults, in ways that we will be examining later in this chapter. But if this idea is new to you, take a pause to process it; this is why some children and people are just so exasperating – they think very differently from me. And if you're finding my style of writing annoying, perplexing or invigorating, that tells you how like, or unlike, my thinking your thinking is!

The modern metaphor favoured for this theory is that of the 'little scientist': someone who is actively exploring the world, seeking understanding and knowledge. Think about a crawling baby: she scours her world, picking up whatever takes her eye and usually putting it into her mouth, the best sense receptor of a small person. If it's not removed by a hovering carer, the child will taste and roll the object around, trying out its surfaces and texture. How does the child know the difference between mashed banana and mashed dirt otherwise? The older child will gaze at new objects, turn them over in his hands, possibly lick them (how efficient was that carer?) and, if the right things are to hand, may well measure or draw them. If I find something new, I will look at it carefully before picking it up, in case it should be something harmful. Many years ago, walking in the Lake District, my husband and I came across a (live) snake on the path. I proceeded to pick it up while he proceeded to endeavour not to panic. I was a biology teacher at the time, and what was critical was not that I recognized the snake but that I picked it up correctly, holding it just behind the head. (It was a grass snake . . .) I was using information that I had internalized at some point in my life. My husband was not party to that information at the time, but he is now! At about the same time, I was head of year at a comprehensive school, in charge of what would now be called Year 12 students. I had a super batch of cheeky special needs lads, who liked practical jokes. One day, I found a dead mouse on my desk in my office. Not being at all squeamish (I was a biology teacher, after all) I picked up the mouse, took it to the special needs room and put it on one of these lads' desks. He thought it was hilarious, and had more respect for me afterwards. He had expected me to act as many people would and to create a huge fuss over a dead mouse. He learned that I wasn't squeamish, and also that I enjoyed a joke.

Piaget thought that a child tries to adapt to the world that he lives in, and that as the child gets older he does it in increasingly successful ways. The process of adaptation takes time, and is made up of several sub-processes, and here we must use some jargon.

A 'scheme' is roughly the same as the word 'concept' – a mental category or complex of ideas. So if you say the word 'dog' to me, I have a clear mental picture, a concept, of what the word 'dog' represents. At the time of writing, I have a dog who clearly is a very doggy dog – lots of children want to stroke him, and tiny children say 'dog' or 'woof' when they see him. Actually, I think he looks more like a Jacob Sheep with a dog's head, but that's a matter of perspective and my confused scheme regarding sheep and shaggy dogs. If you were to say 'black Labrador' then I have an even clearer picture of what you are talking about: I have a concept of dog, which includes black Labradors. My dog is not part of the black Labrador scheme, and never will be.

Piaget takes this a bit further, saying that knowledge is not a passive mental category but actions, either mental or physical, and each of these actions is a scheme. The scheme is not actually the categorization, but the action of categorizing. So when the child looks at my dog, she is using her looking scheme. When she reaches out and grabs a fistful of his lovely woolly coat, she is using her grasping scheme. Babies have a limited repertoire of schemes, but, as you can surmise, this repertoire is added to at an amazing rate and grows very quickly. The crawling toddler knows something by its feel, look and taste. Two years later that same toddler will use very different methods to judge an object.

The word that is used for this intake of knowledge is 'assimilation'. Children assimilate information and incorporate it into their thinking, their schemes. The small toddler who first sees my dog will hear an adult say 'dog' as she reaches out. 'Doggies say woof' may also be there in her environment. So next time, when she is beginning to speak and she sees something like my dog, she'll reach out and say 'dog' or 'woof'. She has assimilated my dog as 'dog'. She may well realize that not all dogs look the same, but there is something she is picking up on – four legs, tail, certain shape head, droopy tongue – that sparks 'dog' internally. Assimilation is an active process, and we select the information that we assimilate. Colour is particularly subjective: if you ask my husband about a particular set of glasses and matching water jug that we were given, he'd say that they were green. I'd say that they were brown. Who can say what colour they really were? But for him, the colour they were had been assimilated into his 'shades of green' scheme, while for me they were in my 'shades of brown' scheme. So we were both right, and both wrong. If only all arguments were so easily solved.

It may be that for my dog to enter a child's 'dog' scheme, the child has to adjust and alter the boundary of 'dog' – four-legged animals with a tail and the right shaped head – to include those with a woolly coat. If this is done, then she has 'accommodated' her scheme: she has changed it to include new information about the attributes of that scheme. Shaggy dogs and short-haired dogs are both still 'dog'. Accommodation is the key to developmental change; it's how we reorganize our thoughts to take in new skills and to change our strategies. It's how our concepts grow and develop, a widening of our thinking, letting new information interplay with what we already have to create something new but recognizable as having grown out of what was there before.

As children learn and develop, they are always working to keep a balance, to keep a world view that makes sense. New data may be accommodated and the scheme grows and develops. But if something comes along which changes the whole thing, then the original scheme may have to be ditched and restarted. It is very like a scientist working on a theory; they will try differ-ent experiments to test the theory. Some data will back up the theory, some will speak against it. Eventually, either the old theory has been effectively proven or a new one forms to re-place it. The critical thing is internal cohesion. Thus the child comes to a point of 'equilibrium', a balance that makes sense. At some point the child will learn that my dog is not a sheep, no matter how profound the resemblance! And, more import-antly, that sheep are not dogs. On my first day as a teacher, I only learned the basic route around school – how to find the rooms I needed: science block, staff room, toilets. As I spent more time in the school I learned more details: where the kids smoked, where the teachers smoked, where the head's study was. I learned which areas were no-through corridors, and retraced my steps to find a real thoroughfare. In my learning of the geography of the school, every time I made mental corrections I was accommodating; every time I decided I was lost, mentally scrubbed the map and started again, I was striving for equilibrium.

Piaget thought that a child operated in a similar way to create coherent, fairly consistent models or theories to live by. However, babies inevitably start with a limited repertoire of schemes, and new data coming up against inadequacies in these schemes force a major upheaval every now and then as the baby grows. Piaget found that these radical reworkings seemed to occur at about the same age in the children that he studied. He saw three major points of change.

The first is at about 18 months. Here there seems to be a shift from the dominance of simple sensory and motor schemes to a child beginning to use the first symbols.

The second is between the ages of 5 and 7, when the child adds a new set of powerful schemes which Piaget called 'operations'. The child can suddenly understand far more abstract and general mental actions, such as mental arithmetic.

The third takes place at adolescence, when the child works out how to 'operate on' ideas as well as objects – the beginning of abstract thought.

Piaget thus gives us four stages:

- sensorimotor, from birth to 18 months;
- preoperational, from 18 months to about 5 years;
- concrete operations, from about 5 years to about 12;
- formal operations, from 12 upwards.

Here the alert reader will think, 'Gosh, that sort of reflects our school ages.' Something was being recognized long before Piaget gave us his theory.

Let's look at these stages in a little more detail.

Sensorimotor

This stage is involved with making sense of the world into which the child has been born. The child assimilates information to the limited array of sensory and motor schemes that she was born with; looking and listening, grasping and sucking, she works to accommodate schemes that come to her through her senses and motor abilities. This age is the starting-point for all cognitive development, and the child lives entirely in the present. She responds to the stimuli that come at her, but does not remember, or plan, or intend. As she goes through life she will begin to change, until she knows that her mother or primary carer will always be the same person (unless dire events have taken place) and her doll is always the same object. Daddy has a deeper voice and dirt isn't as nice to eat as banana, although it gets a much bigger response from Mummy. She's not able to manipulate these images, or use symbols to stand for them. When the ability to manipulate her internal symbols begins to take place it shows that she has reached the next stage.

It's been said, rather unflatteringly (towards the child!), that the thinking of a child at this stage can be likened to that of a dog. It's a form of non-contemplative intelligence. As parents will know, development during this stage can be very fast indeed, often seeming to be in leaps rather than gradual growth.

Research, however, has shown that Piaget may not be totally correct, in that there is now evidence that babies do remember from very early days. They learn how to hold a rattle, and they remember who their carer is very quickly and recognize that person – whether it is shape, voice, smell or a combination. Certainly, modern psychologists think babies are far more sophisticated than Piaget gave them credit for. Critically, all agree that over the second half of a child's second year, the thinking shifts and moves into symbolic thoughts. This coincides with a child beginning to use language as her primary means of communication, and is reflected in the onset of tantrums. It must be said that it is of course very difficult to research young babies as you can only observe – you can't engage them in a dialogue to check out what you have seen, or what you think you've seen. This only comes with the next stage.

Preoperational

This is a delightful stage, when the child isn't having a 'wobbly'. He is using symbols in his thinking, and imagination and creativity are rampant in his play. Children in this stage can turn a cardboard box into a house, a car, a tank. Piles of bricks reach up towards the ceiling; hide-outs are made under the table. A playhouse can see the child inside for hours on end. Children take on roles in their playing – like mummies and daddies – although the children find it very hard to play in role with others if they don't all want the same outcomes! The child has rigid thinking; 'This is what mummies do' will only reflect what that child's mummy does, not a general 'mummy'. A child at this age thinks that everyone sees the world exactly as he does – hence the tantrums when it seems that everyone doesn't. The classic Piaget observation at this age is that if you pour identical amounts of fruit juice into a short fat glass and into a tall thin one, the child just knows that the tall thin one contains more. You could then pour the contents of the tall thin glass into a short fat one, and he will still insist that the tall thin one held more juice. (If you've never observed this, try it! It's quite stunning for an adult to watch this taking place – you simply cannot convince the child that the amount really is the same.) This is the principle of conservation, and it's a concept that children of this age just can't handle. Like-wise, if you show a child a picture of a glass of water, and then draw the outline of a glass on its side and ask the child to draw in the water, he will draw a line at 90 degrees to the glass: he doesn't realize that the water will have come out. This sounds so weird to adults, but it certainly took my son a long time, and lots of wet tablecloths, to recognize how liquids spill.

New research implies that children in this stage are less egotistic than Piaget suggested, but they do indeed struggle with appearance and reality. They cannot predict the actions of others just from observation. Children of this age don't understand that 'you know that I know' or that people are thinking all the time, although they recognize that everyone thinks. This doesn't come until they are moving into the next stage, and this reciprocal thinking is needed for real friendship.

Children in this stage understand that there is a link between emotions and circumstances: 'My dog died, so I'm sad.' They are learning the social rules about self-expression – that throwing a tantrum in Tesco's (or anywhere else) is not acceptable, that it's appropriate to smile if things are going well or are funny, but not if someone is sad. The 'social smile' comes at about age 3, although very small children may have a reflex smile for a camera. Language during this stage is growing increasingly sophisticated, and once it achieves a certain level, using vocabulary such as 'want', 'need', 'think' and 'remember', the child will enter the next stage.

Concrete operations

The child has by now discovered or developed a set of abstract rules or strategies for examining and interacting with the world around her, and these are the concrete operations referred to. An operation for Piaget is a set of powerful abstract internal schemes, many associated with mathematical thinking – addition, multiplication, division, ordering, etc. They are the building blocks of logical thinking, giving the child internal rules about objects and the way that they relate: 3 is always less than 4; houses are more than one storey high; adding gives a bigger number, subtraction a smaller one. So now she can look at a page of sums and have a crucial understanding of what the answers should look like. The child will now understand that dogs come in different shapes and sizes, and while a Labrador is always a dog, dogs aren't always Labradors. Children enjoy 'hands on' learning experiences, and are able to go from this particular experience – 'Look at this river valley. What do we notice?' – to the general – 'So are all river valleys like this?' Children of this age love to count species and enjoy cataloguing. They can't yet handle deductive logic, where you start with a principle and work towards an outcome or an observation, as they cannot imagine what they haven't seen or experienced. The reason this stage is called concrete operations is that the child is working with the concrete – what she can see in front of her. She will enjoy becoming knowledgeable about certain subjects, a classic example being dinosaurs, football or the latest 'boy band', and can tell you all about these things in great depth. She will learn new information about these things very easily – as do we all. Expertise makes a big difference at all ages, and this is the stage where it begins.

Children experience enormous changes as they enter adolescence, and this age varies enormously from child to child. However, by about 12, children will be entering the next stage.

Formal operations

Thinking begins to shift from the concrete to the abstract. What is possible can now be imagined and thought through. The child can now extend his concrete operations and reasoning to include objects or situations that he has not experienced directly. Teenage young people plan their wardrobes without actually being in the cupboard with their clothes. They spend a lot of time thinking about their future life – falling in love, long-term relationships, work and career paths. The most obvious effect for many is the self-consciousness that is typical; suddenly young people are aware of being, and of being observed; 'I know that you know that I know', 'I'm aware of you being aware that I'm aware of you' – the permutations are endless!

They are now able to systematically solve problems. Algebra appears in the maths curriculum, and chemistry involves scientific equations involving atoms and molecules that the children probably will never actually see at all but understand and turn around in their minds.

At one time I found myself teaching secondary science, and frequently heard myself say to children who just couldn't grasp such equations, 'Don't worry, it will come, it will all fall into place one day soon.' And indeed, most times it did – the child would suddenly beam as the penny dropped and it all made sense.

Younger children use inductive logic, based on lots of individual experience and interaction. Older children use deductive logic – 'if this, then that . . .' – a kind of thinking used in many branches of science. Although science is taught at primary schools, deductive logic makes a very different impression and is hugely developed at secondary school. During those first few years at secondary school, children develop and change rapidly, physically, emotionally and mentally. They learn to adapt theories and change what they know and believe to be true or correct, and so they become adults rather than children.

Formal operations demands a different level of thinking processes, and it has been estimated that only about 50 to 60 per cent of 20-year-olds use this style of thinking in an industrialized nation such as the UK, although the more heavily technological the society, the more need for formal operations. It could be that most of the time we simply don't need to be using formal operations – do I want to debate this over the dinner table, or would I rather just chat? And in most of our day-to-day lives we are using concrete operations because that's all we need to use. Some adults never use formal operations; their thinking process never got there and so it has never been developed. This may be because they have limited IQ and do not have the mental ability to move into this style of thinking, or simply that they have not been sufficiently well educated to have that extensive vocabulary. Certainly, formal operations requires an ability to juggle concepts mentally that not all achieve, and language is at the root of that ability.

Critically, we all realize that children grow and develop in a continuous way, not in stages as this implies. The changes are usually gradual, and yet there are clear jumps in development.

Piaget believed that development came through a child's interaction with objects. Lev Vygotsky (1896–1934), a Russian psychologist, believed that children are more affected by social interaction; he claimed that playing with others, be they adults or children, is more important than playing with things or toys. Evidence for this has come from a study where children growing up in larger families were found to be slightly more advanced in their thinking than only children in the way that they handled the concept of a false belief. This came about through the children learning about other people's feelings and reactions on a wider scale than children whose social interaction was limited within the family. Most educational psychologists now agree, and our social interaction with the children in our care is crucial for their development.

Understanding how our children grow and develop is critical if we are to target learning and support the children as they grow and develop. While theories are only ever tools, we wouldn't try and dig the garden without a spade . . . neither would I recommend teaching and working with children without some idea of the processes and changes that are taking place inside the child as we watch, and frequently comment upon, the changes that are external.

Questions for discussion

1 What examples have you noticed of children working in these different styles?

2 How does your group work to expand the children's religious vocabulary as you work with them? How could this be improved?

3 How do you encourage your children to ask difficult questions in an environment that is supportive?

3

Personality

———◆◆◆———

Laura and her parents were walking out of church. 'Mummy, what's Jesus' first name?' asked Laura.

'What do you mean, Jesus' first name?' replied Laura's mum.

'Well, God's called Peter, isn't he, so what's Jesus called?' replied Laura.

'What do you mean, God's called Peter?' queried Laura's mum.

'He's got to be called Peter – we say, "Thanks, Peter God", don't we?' replied Laura.

Having spent time thinking about how a child develops intellectually, we need to consider how a child's personality develops. Personality is a difficult concept – what makes me me, and you you? Why is everyone different personality-wise as well as in appearance? If we believe that every person is a gift of God and made in God's image, then personality is a serious issue and worth spending some time thinking over.

Personality is to do with the way that we all, children and adults, go about relating to the people and objects in the world around us. There are differences, and these differences are enduring. I like horses and always have done, you may not. Why do I like horses? Well, I could tell you why, but actually I liked them before I could tell you why – I was just born like that . . . perhaps. You might like to spend a moment now thinking about the qualities that people have. Are they gregarious or shy, independent or dependent? Are they confident or uncertain? You get the drift.

Researchers refer to 'the big five' personality traits: extroversion, agreeableness, conscientiousness, neuroticism and openness–intellect.

Extroversion

This is perhaps the easiest to understand; it's the extent to which someone engages with the world and social experiences. Extrovert people are gregarious and throw themselves into life. They tend to be active, assertive, enthusiastic, outgoing and talkative. Introverts tend towards the opposite, taking time to adapt to new situations and being thoughtful and quiet. Interestingly, some people don't recognize themselves within this spectrum. A quick rule of thumb is that extroverts tend to speak before they think while introverts think before they speak. Extroverts gain energy from being with people, introverts from being on their own.

Agreeableness

Agreeableness is the extent to which a person's nature could be characterized by warmth and compassion, making up an affectionate, forgiving and generous nature. The opposite is an antagonistic person, less trusting and tending to be unkind. An agreeable person may also be gullible and easily 'conned'.

Conscientiousness

Conscientiousness speaks of the extent and strength of a person's impulse control; how able are they to delay gratification, or does it have to be 'now!'? Conscientious people are efficient planners who are reliable and resourceful, thorough in the way that they work and live.

Neuroticism

This is about emotional stability, the extent to which the person experiences the world as worrying or distressing. Is the world a threatening place to be? Neurotic people tend to be touchy and irritable, tense and unstable.

Openness–intellect

This reflects the depth and complexity of a person's mental and experiential life. It includes how creative or artistic the person is, how imaginative they are and how able to communicate that internal vision.

Each personality factor has two sides; for example the opposite of extrovert is introvert. Everyone has the two sides; but will usually operate using their preferred side. So while I'm an extrovert, I sometimes operate as an introvert – taking time out on my own, reflecting internally at meetings to ensure I've thought before I speak, etc. This is referred to as 'using your shadow side' or 'working with your shadow side'. If you are 100 per cent one or the other, you will find it very hard to stand in someone else's shoes or to predict how they will behave or react, so this is a (hard) skill that is worth practising from time to time.

The question for us is: how much of the above is true for children? How much develops later on in life, as opposed to being what we are born with, or develops rapidly as a response to the environment in which we are raised?

Certainly, these traits can be seen in older children and adolescents. Conscientiousness is the trait that is most clearly carried through – children who score highly on the conscientiousness trait tend to do well in school, but that's hardly surprising. Some psychologists would add two more traits: irritability and activity; these are self-explanatory. Many younger children have high activity scores and find it difficult to work at school 'inside their head' rather than in an experiential manner.

Is temperament the same as personality? Temperament would seem to be the substrate of personality, lying beneath the surface and easily spotted if you dig in. The combination of the five traits would seem to be the mix from which the adult personality develops. But, as with adult personality, this is not fixed. Adults can work on their personality and develop sides of their personality as they choose, working on the shadow side, and so can children and young people. Personality would seem to be the result of temperament being worked upon by the environment in which the child is growing. If a child is very active, moving a lot and frequently, there is a high chance that he will grow into an extrovert adult with a high sociability factor. There are also links between extroversion and agreeableness, but this could be because extroverts gain their acceptance from others rather than from within themselves.

Children who are inhibited as toddlers often grow into shy children and adults. They may respond with fear or withdrawal from new people or experiences, the opposite of the extrovert pattern of behaviour. These children may have higher scores on the neuroticism trait later in life. These may be the children who become angry, fussy, loud or irritable as they go through school – the classic 'difficult child'. If skilled people can help them to control their difficulties and stay focused, managing their attention and effort, they will become more conscientious and grow more open to new experiences.

It is very important for us to realize that what is acceptable, normal, in one culture may not be so in another. A friend who has a very active son went to live in the USA while he was primary school age. A child English teachers had seen as quite a demanding pupil, for he was also very bright, became a joy for American teachers working in a culture where children are encouraged to be more expressive than English children typically are.

Research is indicating that a child's temperament will persist into adulthood as her personality. Babies who have a positive approach to the world tend to keep that positive outlook. Difficult babies tend to show that difficulty ten years later. Strongly inhibited babies tend to become shy adults.

The characteristics of a baby's temperament interact with the child's environment to either strengthen or modify that child. Parental response can make a huge difference to modifying a baby's temperament by their handling of the child. If parents are warm towards their child, the child will learn to be warm in the interaction with others too. If they are cold and distant, that will be the way that the child handles other people's approaches. If a shy child is encouraged to take part in the world and shown that she can indeed do that, then she will become less shy. If parents simply say, 'Oh, she's shy,' and leave the child to hide behind them, then the child may still be hiding behind them in the years to come.

Most children's temperaments fall within the mid-range of the spectrum, and these children will adapt to their environments. Children with extreme temperaments may force their environment to adapt to them, so a difficult child will be scolded more often, and will have more negative reinforcement coming to him. He will have less support from his parents than a child who is less bother (but he will gain the attention that he may crave). Children with difficult temperaments are also likely to display emotional difficulties and difficult behaviour patterns. Sensitive parents can modify and moderate these more difficult patterns of behaviour, but it is demanding work, as the glut of nannying and parenting TV programmes can show us. If behaviour is reinforced in a partial way then the behaviour will probably get worse – that 'naughty step', once decided on, must be carried through. 'Lifting' strategies with children who are wakeful at night can often work amazingly quickly if the strategy is adhered to.[1]

Poor parental discipline for any child reaps problems later on in the child's life. It is even possible for parents to create a system at home where the children are actually in charge of the parents.

Twin studies indicate that some element of personality is inherited; studies done of twins growing up apart are well known. When twins who had never met were brought together, some were wearing identical clothes, had identical haircuts and enjoyed the same activities. A Jewish friend once observed to me that God sends us the children we can least cope with, in that they remind us of ourselves! Certainly, the traits that I found most difficult in my daughter as a child were the ones that were like watching myself! Children do seem to be like walking re-incarnations of their parents, grandparents, etc. and whether that is us projecting on to them or they really are like that person is hard to disentangle. Certainly if you are a parent, you will have observed your parents' traits in your children and wondered how they got there!

I come down on the side of some genetic inheritance and some environment. Nature is combined with nurture for almost all of us.

The most important comment to make with regard to these difficult areas is that modelling always reaps more rewards than preaching. If we show children through our lives and actions what we expect of them, they will indeed start to behave in what we regard as a 'better' way. Better for us, and better for them. But to tell children how to behave and then not carry that out in our lives is inconsistent; children will always do as we do, not as we say.

Personality type indicators

Many adults reading this book will have used various tools that are now available to classify their own personality type.

Probably the most popular of these at present is the Myers–Briggs personality type indicator. This system, which classifies people into one of 16 types, was devised following basic Jungian typology and Jung's understanding of how people flourish. Myers and Briggs took the four Jungian aspects of personality and combined them, giving 16 different types. Two of the aspects are processes, one aspect is to do with attitude, and the fourth concerns orientation.

The process options relate to situations and how we handle them. They are Sensing versus iNtuition and Thinking versus Feeling. The attitude measure is Judgment versus Perception, and the orientation is Extroversion versus Introversion. The combinations are listed by the capital letters – for example, ENFJ, ISTF – and indicate the person's preferred way of acting, although this does not mean that he never uses his shadow side. So while I am usually an extrovert, from time to time I enjoy time on my own, thinking things through. But after a day in front of my square screen I am keen to meet someone for a chat and social interaction!

Each type will show a very different personality and way of carrying out their lives and work. What it is critical for us to note is that this system can help me to see why that person drives me round the bend; I can then work to understand why she is acting in the way that she is, and realize that I am probably equally annoying and difficult for her. Once again, we see that everyone really is unique: she is not likely to think or act as I do, and neither of those ways will necessarily be The Right Way. There is a real need to live and let live.

Table 3.1 summarizes the differences. If you find this interesting, you can find a basic test on the Internet, which will help you label yourself, but you may find a day with an accredited Myers–Briggs specialist rather more helpful. Churches often have a Myers–Briggs workshop for their new church council. Over time, personality indicators can vary. When I was previously

Table 3.1

How do you prefer to process information? S or N	
Sensing	*iNtuition*
Facts, multi-sensory	Abstract, image
Actual, definite, authentic	Inspiration, impression, potential

How do you prefer to make decisions? T or F	
Thinking	*Feeling*
Logical analysis	Personal consequences
Issues rather than feelings	Principles may be overlooked
Justice, acting on what's fair – consequently others' feelings may get hurt	Sympathy overrides

How do you deal with the external world? E or I	
Extrovert	*Introvert*
External world, public, social	Tend to be in my inner world, private person
Gregarious, groups are energizing	I find solitude refreshing
I tend to speak before I think	I tend to think before I speak

How do you like to organize your life? J or P	
Judgment	*Perception*
Ordered, planned	Open, flexible to new ideas/ approaches
Like closure, lists welcomed	I look for further information and other possibilities
I favour coming to clear decisions	Final decisions are often postponed

tested, I was just an F, by about three responses. Recently I was tested again, and my indicator had moved, by just a few responses, to T. This was because I had needed to operate with the shadow side (T) and that had become my preferred modus operandi in that indicator area. Thus my preference was reflected in my indicator switching from F to T. You can work on your shadow side to try and bring it into play more often, and if you are working with a similar type person it's sometimes fun to stop and think how someone who has a very different way of interacting with your world would react to what you are planning!

It's also important to recognize that with different personality types come different preferences for worship. Different prayer styles, different types of music . . . there really isn't a 'right' way to pray, I'm afraid, just the right way for you. So variety really is the spice of life here! And remember – you aren't 'stuck' with this type for life; if there's something you don't like about your personality, get on with changing it by consciously getting yourself to use your shadow more often.

There is no 'better' type either – just how people are. You will prefer certain types, as they affirm you as a person and the way you set about doing things, but life would be boring if we didn't have heated discussions, wouldn't it?

As with temperament, children can be seen to be developing these traits as they mature. The trick is to aim towards a balance; so while adults will always fall into one or other of these groups, if their score is near the boundary they are more balanced individuals.

Another aspect that will affect a child is that of the psychoemotional growth that we each undergo. This was studied by Erik Erikson (1902–94), who developed a scheme that helps us to understand another aspect of what is going on in a person's life. Erikson practised as an analyst, and his system is again very helpful as we work with children, to give us a tool to try and understand the stresses and strains that our children are working on at any one time.

For about the first year of life, the child is engaged in *basic trust versus basic mistrust*, where the child is learning to trust her mother or chief carer and learning about her own ability to make things happen: Mum arrives if I cry, talks to me and smiles in response to my smile; she continues to exist even when

I can't see her, and always reacts to me in (roughly) the same way, with care and concern.

From about 2 to 3, we see *autonomy versus shame*. The child is now mobile, and her physical freedoms lead to her exercising free choice. She will go through toilet training, and her increasing sense of self-esteem will give her a lasting sense of pride and goodwill. If, however this self-esteem is not there, because the child is being shamed and has self-doubts, the seeds of low self-esteem are sown and may be hard to overcome. Her internal sense of justice also develops through her sense of autonomy.

At about the age of 4 to 5, the child enters the stage called *initiative versus guilt*. At this age he likes to organize his activities around clearly defined goals. He loves to work with other children, and learns rapidly – that 'sponge-like' quality that is so attractive. There may be conflict with the same-sex parent, and this can lead to feelings of guilt in the growing child.

From about 6 to 12 years, the child is engaged in *industry versus inferiority*, working to absorb the norms of the culture in which she lives. All children engage in some learning at this point, no matter where they live. They are very concerned to make things – think of all those box sculptures that infant children bring home from school, the pictures on the fridge, and the storybooks of the older child. Their more aggressive drives go into a more dormant state, and they may become very conformist.

From 13 to 18 years, the adolescent period, the young person is in the stage called *identity versus role confusion*. There are many tasks for adolescents to deal with: adapting to the physical changes that take place; making an occupational choice, or at least choosing where to study further; achieving an adult sexual identity and searching for new values which they feel are 'theirs' and not those of the people among whom they've been living since birth. They may have to go through the fights of early childhood once more, with parents playing their adversary, albeit unwillingly. They take on idols, icons and ideas as they move towards this more lasting identity, trying to integrate their personalities, taking from their childhood as well as the people among whom they now socialize. They may over-identify with certain groups, joining cliques or gangs as they express themselves over and against the child they were. These young people will fall in love, while the sexual mores of the culture will determine how active they are sexually. They are also developing their own set of ethics and morality, and tend to believe that really successful adults are also the 'best' adults.[2]

Learning styles

This section of the chapter is entirely based on adult styles of learning. However, children are learning and laying down their basic approach to life, and in the same way that their temperament will give a clue to adult personality, so adult approaches to learning will give a clue retrospectively as to how children are learning. Watch a group of children and you can see the different styles developing very young: for example, there are the children who don't do jigsaws and others who prefer to sit and concentrate, the child playing on his own, entirely caught up in a different world, while others play as a gang . . . Different learning-styled people like to learn in different ways, and adults can be separated into four preferred styles of learning.

Activists

These are people who like a challenge. They think variety is the spice of life, hope that learning is going to be enjoyable and don't mind making mistakes. Activists are bored quickly and 'turn off'. They can be quite difficult and challenging people to have in a group, as they will want it to move along at a good pace. They will have an extrovert personality.

An activist will approach learning with these questions:

- Will I learn something new?
- Will there be a mixture of things to do? I do not want to sit for hours at a time doing nothing.
- Will I be tied down to one particular subject or method, or are there options?
- Will there be some tough challenges for me to meet so I do not feel as if I am wasting my time?
- Will there be people like me on the course?

Reflectors

Reflectors don't like pressure or being in the spotlight. They may not be good at giving instant responses to groups or exercises, as they like to hear other people's views. They will have an introvert personality. A reflector will approach learning with these questions:

- Will I be given time to prepare and think things through properly or will I be put on the spot?
- Will there be a chance to do things properly, getting relevant information and thinking things out as we go along, or will it be all slapdash?
- Will we be steamrollered along a particular line, not encouraged to think for ourselves but given answers and information we have no opportunity to question?
- Will I get a chance to hear views of others in the group?
- If I am working alone, will I get enough time to do things properly? Do I have the support and encouragement of anyone outside the course?

Theorists

Theorists like being intellectually stretched and thrive on argument and discussion. They want to explore the structure of things, the theoretical base and the thinking behind taken-for-granted assumptions. They may be either extrovert or introvert. A theorist will approach learning with these questions:

- Will I have a chance to question what's going on?
- Can the leaflet in front of me or the tutor of the course give me a clear idea of what we are going to learn, how we are going to learn it and why?
- Is this course going to be too easy for me? Or will I only encounter ideas and arguments with which I am already familiar?
- Will there be people with my interests and approach there?

Pragmatists

Pragmatists are more likely to learn from successful people who have proved their competency in the field than from ivory-towered experts. Again, they may be either extrovert or introvert. A pragmatist will approach learning with these questions:

- Will there be lots of practical tips and techniques?
- Will there be opportunities to practise?
- Have the people running the course shown that they know how to do this themselves?
- Is this course or event tackling real problems and some of my current concerns, which are . . .

These learning styles are found in adults, but recently there has been a great deal of interest shown in children's learning styles. The DfES now recommend that children are taught in a variety of styles but do not use the four classifications above. Instead, teachers now refer to VAK: visual, auditory and kinaesthetic learning styles. Children who prefer visual learning would benefit from old-fashioned 'chalk and talk' where the information is displayed and the teacher takes the child through it. Worksheets, reference books and even the Internet are all examples of visual learning. Auditory learners focus on the sound of the lesson, be it from the teacher or something recorded, with the visual input less important. A kinaesthetic learner learns best when something active is involved, for example, role-play. These children often find it hard to write up work or to concentrate for long periods with a book.

VAK may relate to the four adult styles, the most obvious parallel being kinaesthetic relating to activist. There is still some debate over the value of the VAK system, but for me the important fact is that children, like adults, learn best when the material is presented in a varied manner. This way, each learning style is catered for and the learners all have to use the styles that they may not prefer, helping them to have a balance and to also use the shadow styles.

Questions for discussion

1 What personality type are you? If you don't know, why not try out a Myers–Briggs workshop together? They're great fun as well as very helpful.

2 Do you have a favourite type of child – quiet, boisterous, outgoing, shy? Can you say what it is about that type of child that you enjoy?

3 (Something to do alone.) What aspect of your personality do you dislike the most? What can you work on to help it to change? How will you pray about this?

4 How do you decide on the worship that your children experience? Should you widen the methods that you are using?

4

Social development

*I think about God when I'm scared like the time my dad told me
to go downstairs and my brother scared me.*

(Isabella, 6)

This chapter is about the skills that we all learn, some during
our childhood and some as we grow older. Some social skills
are picked up in later life. For us, the important thing to recognize is that we do indeed learn these skills, even though we will
have no memory of so doing. For us as adults, working with
children, we need to be aware that we may have expectations
that are totally at odds with some of our children's life experience, and this will affect how we interact with our young charges.
Our expectations are deep-seated and 'invisible' a great deal of
the time; it is only when we realize we are finding a particular
child (or adult) difficult that we stand back, analyse what's going
on here, and recognize the disjunction between us. So let's consciously think about some of these invisible factors that may
be at work.

Socialization

Socialization is one of those things that you're only aware of
when it goes wrong: a bit like your central heating system. And
like that central heating, socialization often breaks down at
Christmas! Socialization refers to the system by which we pick
up the normal way of behaving. It's usually unnoticed and always
assumed to be common to all in a group, and it's only when

someone goes beyond or outside the rules of the group that we become aware of the subtle processes that keep society and groups together. We learn rules of behaviour such as not speaking over other people, not leaving a restaurant without paying the bill, not throwing rubbish on the floor, remembering to wipe feet or remove shoes on entering a house . . . and you can't remember how you did that learning. You 'just know'. We usually conform to group norms without noticing that they are there. Some people clearly find it easier to speak out against a group than others; those who chair committees will be aware of that, and we all know such people, and may quietly envy them their 'thick skin' when it comes to saying what they think despite the feeling that the rest of the group have – or have gone along with. Likewise, we have all been in a group where there is a newcomer who doesn't know how the group works and may speak and act in a way that we find disturbing, but cannot quite articulate why. Unless that person works out the difference, they may find themselves being quietly, and probably unintentionally, squeezed out.

Does this conformity come from that most ancient of causes, survival instinct? I think it does. If a pack or herd animal is alone, outside of the group, it is likely to be picked off by a predator, and eaten. And those who are outside of the dominant social group of humans are just as likely to be picked upon and 'devoured' by the big people who set the rules of what is 'normal'. We see it in nurseries, where some children are excluded from the group, often for reasons adults cannot fathom at all. As children move up through the school they may have the wrong type of school jumper. We know about designer trainers and so forth. I can remember a girl when I was about 9 whom we ostracized because she was 'square'; she had absolutely no fashion sense at all, nor did she conform to many of the other social mores that our group held. Adults are not above this sort of behaviour: colour, sexuality, gender, slavery – all of these were legal distinctions until strong people stood up against the crowd. Many are still discriminated against in the wider population, with subtle behaviours that continue unless challenged either internally by the conscience or externally by someone speaking out. Your church will have different groups too, where people with the same interests and lifestyles tend to group. You know – the 'choir group', the 'servers' group', possibly the 'Sunday school teachers' group' . . .

Groupthink

People who challenge the social norms are standing against a factor called 'groupthink'. I know it sounds like something from Orwell's *1984* but it's a powerful force, and one to be recognized and reckoned with. Groupthink is the social pressure to conform to what a group is thinking. So if you go to a BNP rally, it's hard to speak of an inclusive multi-cultural country in a positive light. If you're at a black-tie dinner, chances are you're wearing a rather swanky suit or a posh frock. My husband took great delight in not wearing a tie to a Buckingham Palace garden party (one of the perks of my present post) but I didn't see any women in trousers, although a few (clergy) men were wearing frocks!

Although I'm joking here about groupthink, it's a very strong force. Perhaps the worst example I know is from the committee that met to decide whether to launch a certain space shuttle on a very frosty morning. The ice caused an 'O-ring' to fail, and the shuttle, *Challenger*, exploded on launch. One man alone said this would happen and desperately tried to persuade the others on the launch committee to postpone. As you know, all on board that shuttle died, and the programme was grounded for years as a result.

Groupthink often means that a group of individuals agree together to do something that none of them would even con-sider on their own. Ever find yourself wondering just how you agreed to do that task at the last church meeting? Was this how you became Sunday school superintendent, or whatever you call that role in your church?

Freud held that socialization was achieved through the repression of children, forcing them to conform to the roles and norms of adults. This is not generally held to be so, but some socialization certainly can be repressive. The film *School of Rock* gives a great example of a very smart American private school accidentally employing a rock guitar player, and how his encouraging the children to play rock music rather than classical helps them to break out of the repressive expectations of their parents. Don't get me wrong, I love classical music, but a good blast of Led Zeppelin[1] works differently on the psyche. And those kids needed to let their hair down and enjoy being what they were – kids.

Children do not have an innate working model of the society into which they have been born. It is clearly up to others to teach them. How deep that teaching goes is questionable, as is seen in books such as *Lord of the Flies*,[2] or what we see happening in states of war. However, in 'normal' times, societies exist and are clearly different across the globe. A multinational bank runs TV advertisements about what is acceptable in one culture being unacceptable in others – it's one of the joys of foreign travel. It seems to me that only people who speak English as a second language reply 'You're welcome' when I thank them! Each culture has its own ways of being and doing. The recent novel *One Big Damn Puzzler*[3] gives a brilliant insight into a foreigner living and working abroad. One of the norms was you shouldn't share a house with anyone of the opposite sex if you weren't married. Sex outside marriage was rife, but they never stayed for breakfast with their lovers . . .

Research into socialization

It was the advent of video recording that gave those researching social development the biggest leap forward, as children could now be watched without setting up laboratory conditions, which nearly always give skewed results. As a result of this, the 'mutuality' model[4] was proposed. This says that children are active participants in their own social development, stressing their *inter-*dependence with their adult carer for many of their social interactions. While adults like to think they're teaching the child, the child actually has more control in this process than we recognize. But note – no researcher has ever said that there won't be stresses and conflicts during this process. Tantrums are official! Through a whole gamut of exploration and stimuli, the child learns and progresses socially. Children are not a blank slate at birth; they bring their own predispositions, capacities and reflexes. Any parent will tell you that his or her children were born with the makings of the person they become, that all children, even identical twins, are very different. One may have a 'laid-back' personality in contrast to big sister's much more 'up and at 'em' approach to life. So while children respond to the people and the world around them, they do it from varying starting positions.

All children are particularly tuned in to other human beings. Put a child in the room, and he will go to the people rather than the library books – often taking an adult to the books, but finding the person first. Children prefer people who talk and move to those who sit like a statue in silence (don't we all!). That's why babies seem to almost expect to be entertained by adults. That's what we do automatically.

We are all predisposed to prefer human voices to any other sounds, and adults will tune in to a small child before a larger one. Bring a newborn into a room and watch everyone, men and children included, focus on the child. We can't help it! And, as we get older, we maintain the tendency to see faces in many things; look at the 'I saw Jesus in my beer foam' stories in the press, the faces you see before you go to sleep.

See how we hold young babies too – at face-to-face level, which actually gives a fairer power dynamic. We are looking straight into the baby's eyes, but she can turn her head away if she so desires, and make us work to catch her attention. If you watch the way adults talk to babies, you may notice the way that by about 6 months the child is being given a space to reply, even though she doesn't speak. Chatting in this way with very small children gives children the turn-taking practice that will enable conversation later on.

Development of relationships

John Donne commented that 'No man is an Island, entire of itself' and he was absolutely right. We are always searching for other people. Human beings are relational beings, and that is the interpretation many modern theologians have of being made in the image of God. How those relationships develop has been studied carefully. The first relationships that we develop will be with those who care for us, and as we go through life the quality of those first relationships will affect the quality of ones that we form later. So you really can blame your parents! A specific, enduring tie between two humans is called an 'attachment', and with young children evidence of an attachment is given through the child preferring that person's attention, touching, clinging to them, crying for them if they're not there, smiling at them when they are. You will instinctively recognize when that relationship is healthy, and likewise alarm bells will ring when you see a parent and child who do not share a healthy relationship. Our first attachment can be observed very early on, but from six months it is quite marked. It's necessary at the start of life, or who would feed, care for and protect this young person?

Animals clearly exhibit attachments in the same way as humans. Emperor penguins and sea horses are known for the extreme parenting skills of the male. Elephants have been known to remain in the area where their young perished and attack the object that caused the death, as in the fairly recent case where a baby elephant was killed by a train and the mother 'haunted' that area of track, causing mayhem in her grief. But few animals care for their young in the extended way that humans do. There are few species that care for more than one birth's worth of offspring alongside each other without forcing the older to leave.

All over the world, researchers have recognized three different styles of attachment; I use 'mother' here to represent the key carer, but clearly it may be other people who are significant in the child's rearing.

Anxious–avoidant

A child who has this type of attachment will show little distress when her mother leaves, and shows equally little interest when her mother returns. Approximately 20 per cent of the population exhibits this style.

Securely attached

In these cases, the child actively seeks to maintain proximity to her mother. When her mother is present, the child will actively explore and interact with other people and objects. She will be distressed if her mother departs, and will greet her mother enthusiastically on return. Seventy per cent of the population demonstrate this style of attachment.

Anxious–ambivalent

This child shows distress when her mother leaves, but will resist contact when she returns and may display anger during their reunion. Ten per cent of the population exhibit this style. (But about 75 per cent of the characters in the soap operas we know and love so well have the less stable attachment styles. Otherwise there wouldn't be the same amazing storylines.)

There is much evidence that it is to the individual's advantage to have the second style of attachment. These people score higher on tests in interpersonal confidence and cognitive development, play more with toys, explore more willingly and in a healthier manner and show a greater eagerness to learn. The provision of a secure base in this first relationship has implications for later relationships. We continue to form attachments right throughout our life, and they are important to us; the pattern of our early relationships will become the model for those we form later on.

Expectations of relationships vary with the original style of attachment. Anxious–ambivalent adults are more uncertain about their relationships, and may worry that their partner doesn't love them. This can lead to the breakdown of the partnership, not helped by their own inconsistent displays of emotion. Avoidant lovers will find any close relationship uncomfortable and they will be reluctant to commit.

When we look at people's orientation towards society, we discover that the quality of attachment towards a father will affect how patriotic a child may become. Those with a secure attachment will love their country, but an insecure attachment will give a child a tendency towards preoccupation with national dominance. Perhaps of most interest to this book, some research implied that the quality of this first attachment will give differing styles of religious commitment,[5] in that those with secure attachment will find it easier to have a good understanding of God, whereas those with less security may have an exclusive 'me and God' style of faith which is very critical of ministers and the church community.

Other research showed that those with a secure attachment coped with trauma by seeking help from others, while those who were ambivalent would become emotionally volatile, and the avoidants would try to distance themselves psychologically from events.

The development of language

Inevitably, there is a great deal of interest in the way we develop language. Clearly a very sophisticated process is taking place, and children take quite a while to pick up grammar as well as vocabulary. A toddler will presume how to make a plural of a word, saying 'mouses' or 'mans' rather than 'mice' and 'men'. He will say that he 'runned' rather than 'ran'; it can be quite difficult to get children to use the correct, acceptable form of the language. There is no doubt that what they learn is related to a specific context and social experiences; a child will not offer vocabulary to do with an office block unless she has experienced either a book or a story about this, has been taken there or has somehow come across that environment. Likewise, a child in the UK is not likely to know about life in Ancient Rome unless he has been specifically told about it. Children pick up intonation, vocabulary, phrasing and accent from the people they hear speaking, and this can be very specific to a small area.

Children learn about reciprocity – taking it in turns to produce a conversation – early in their lives. This pattern gives rise to dialogue, but small children can find 'waiting their turn' very difficult.

Parents work hard with their child giving vocabulary and language within a shared context. How many hours do most parents spend reading to their child, so increasing their vocabulary and knowledge of speech? It has been observed that parents will take a lead on their subject matter by monitoring the interest level of the child. Mine loved to talk about all sorts of things, but the finer detail of theology had to wait a while . . . Carers will also give a format for language: for example, in reading a picture book the adult will point and say, 'That's a boat, that's a car, that's a train,' with the 'that's a' working as a signal each time that the really important word, the noun, is the one to learn, as that's the one that changes as the picture changes. Carers will also unconsciously be monitoring the level of interest that the child shows as she chats, and will skew the conversation towards the subjects that the child is interested in – so if a child is playing with her trains, that's what the carer will chat about. If the carer is talking to the child about the dog and a horse trots by, catching the child's attention, then the chat will shift to horses, and so on.

You will have noticed that we use a different tone of voice when speaking to young children. We raise the pitch, we speak more slowly and we change the emphasis. This can be called 'parentese' or child-addressed speech. I'm afraid I use the same style with my dog . . . But we simplify the language and so simplify the task of learning, just as I would do if I ever had to teach a language to a non-speaker. I don't want to learn French from someone speaking at their normal speed and using all sorts of complicated grammatical structure; '*Jean écoute la radio*', slowly and precisely, will do! Likewise, it's thought that children acquire the framework for language before vocabulary.

There are clearly some problems with the above theory. I speak parentese to my dog, and while he's got me well trained to understand certain looks (he's waiting for tea as I type, and we both know that I know what he wants!) he's never opened his mouth and asked me, 'Please could I have tea now?' And while some birds can copy words – no examples here for obvious reasons – they never come out with words in a sentence unless they've been drilled previously.

Children all seem to learn language at about the same time no matter where they live. So a Russian toddler will be making the same sorts of babbling noises as the toddler in our local deli, but while the Russian child will speak Russian, our deli toddler will speak English, with a smattering of Greek and Italian. But there has yet to be a toddler who could speak who grew up in isolation. We need others around us to model how to do it. Tarzan had to learn how to say 'Me Tarzan, you Jane' as an adolescent.

There is a huge debate about how we learn to speak, and it's now believed by many that we are born to speak, as we are born to walk upright. What we learn is the language and dialect of speech, but that speech is somehow now instinctive.

Acquiring language is a truly stunning feat, one that we have all mastered without thinking about it. While I may wish I had a wider vocabulary, I manage to communicate well enough. And here's an obvious comment that you may not have thought of before: language is a tool. If you don't use it, it is useless! A conversation is an amazing social interaction of expression and impression. Think of the conversations you've had today. Sometimes we do have to reiterate as we've rushed on to the point without keeping our audience with us, but overall – isn't it stunning? Language is a task that we have never come to the end of; think of all those words you don't know! We continue learning throughout our lives, not only technical jargon that's still being invented, but the rich vocabulary in which we are immersed. Language is the medium through which we teach, tell stories, we ask and answer questions, we assert our authority, we say what's what and whose coat that is . . . and while the style of our language informs other listeners a great deal about us, without language we would not be doing what we do for so much of the time.

You will have noticed, too, how quickly accents change when families move area; my children were born in Nottingham, and had hard vowel sounds until we moved to Hertfordshire. Within a few months, my daughter was posh estuary, though my son took longer to stop saying 'one' in the northern manner. When we moved round London to Kent, the accent switched oh so subtly to Kent estuary English. Now my son is in York, I wonder what he'll sound like soon! Listen to me speak, and you'll probably ask me where I come from, for I have a north Midland vowel sound that just comes through from time to time, though I can't hear it. My first teaching job was in a mining area of Nottinghamshire. I lived in the city and had no problem with that accent at all, but when I started in this particular school I thought I'd entered a foreign country. When I asked a child where his homework was, he replied, 'It's a tom' (It's at home). It took me weeks to pick up this very local but very dense accent. The children thought I was French, because the other teacher without a local accent was actually German, and my name sounded foreign. And we are not alone. The Queen has also come downmarket in her accent over the 50 years of Christmas broadcasts. Gangs use language to set them apart, with their own 'in-house' dialect. And I won't go into texting!

Our understanding of the world is affected by our understanding of our language. We cannot overestimate how critical it is. Many years ago I worked in a UPA (Urban Priority Area) with young people and adults' groups. One of the women's groups had a crèche, with qualified speech therapists. The local schools were finding the children in their nursery class and upwards violent, and it was realized that it was because the children found communication hard with their teachers. They couldn't articulate their needs through recognized speech, so speech therapists were trying to provide a richer language environment for these children. This was a case of proactive therapy, to save more expensive intervention later on.

This raises a very important area for us as communicators: there are many forms of speech, and we all tend to believe that we do it properly. Thus if a child comes to Sunday school and is silent, it may not be because she has a poor command of English; it may be that her English is different from mine. Put her into a safe environment and she'll chatter away happily. The language I'm using is different from that of her home environment, and that does not make mine correct and hers wrong – they are just different. We will need time together to come to a compromise, and we'll do it without noticing.

Body language

While verbal language is crucial, it's said that only 10 per cent of communication is spoken – the rest is taken in subconsciously through body language. Most of us are now familiar with the basic concept of body language – that we speak far more loudly with our bodies than we do with our mouths, and that we are subconsciously responding to someone's body language all the time. Take a standard situation: Suzie has been naughty, and you are about to tell her off. You'll take a deep breath, and your body will expand. You may cross your arms, and Suzie will see this, and mentally brace herself before you've opened your mouth. Or you're going to praise Suzie for her fantastic story: you'll smile, right up to your eyes, and possibly lean back, or to one side. Again, Suzie knows what's coming before you open your mouth. Watch a couple of women in a coffee shop as they chat. (Sorry, but women do this better than men, as a generalization.) They will lean in towards each other, and their bodies will tend to mirror each other. Their heads could be quite close together . . . and off they go, taking turns and just sensing when it's their turn to join in. I once sat in a clergy meeting with the local MP, who was a cabinet minister at the time. I could not work out why something was ringing alarm bells in my head until quite a while afterwards; what he said was OK, he seemed nice enough . . . and then I realized that he had been sitting in a perfectly body-neutral manner, legs straight out in front, feet flat on the floor, hands on knees, and he hadn't moved. There was no body language coming from him, and he felt like a talking dummy. We need body language to give us the rest of the story. Deaf people who lip-read say that they need to be face on to 'see' the words, but the real story is in the rest of my body as we talk to each other.

Like language and dialect, body language is localized. I know that a Greek person is likely to be far more bodily active when I chat with him. Italians – well, they like to be dramatic, as do Spaniards; gross generalizations here, but you get my drift. But if you are talking with someone from another culture, it could be that your body language confuses her, as one gesture may have a very different overtone in her language or dialect; pointing fingers is a prime example. So do be aware that someone coming into your group from outside the area may be struggling to get up to speed with body language just as much as verbalization.

Understanding people and society

If we are to function within society, we need to be able to take in all sorts of information about the other people among whom we are working and living. Every child needs to grasp that people are unique; everyone is different and will react differently. We all look different, too, and we have a store of recognition data to enable us to recognize the right person before we throw ourselves into their arms. Have you experienced that lovely moment of having a toddler attach himself to you, look up and realize that you're the wrong pair of legs? How do I learn who has the same sense of humour as I have? This is vital knowledge if I'm not to really get it wrong socially, as where to draw the line is a very variable point. We cannot observe mental activity, just its merest glimmerings on another person's face, but a toddler soon learns how to read that face. Children learn to watch and read non-verbal language at a very early age, and to gauge what's going on beneath the surface. We still do not understand how we acquire this understanding, but it seems that younger children read physical appearance more than older children, who will speak about personality rather than physical descriptions.

During middle childhood the understanding of these fine mechanisms increases, and the concept of friends, friendships and mutual responsibilities and the obligations of peers develops. Children as young as 5 can predict how people they know well will respond, which shows an understanding that other people are thinking, remembering and perceiving. Learning this skill seems to depend on the child's social context and listening to other people speaking about their own social interactions. As the child grows older, so the awful reality of social embarrassment appears. It seems almost as if the parent and the child are one unit, as a parent's embarrassment will lead to the child sharing the emotion. Much of this social embarrassment can be seen in situations where other people are thinking that 'the child should know better'; those of us with tall children will know the feeling well. I remember taking a christening where the child, who was very big for his age and running at 11 months, was appallingly behaved – for a 2- or 3-year-old. When people realized he wasn't even a year old, they rapidly revised their opinions. Well, some did.

Children also have to learn all about the social structures of their culture. It's within their family that they learn about religion and faith life lived in the community. It's their families that teach them about shops and how they work, with many children believing that there's no end to the money in that machine in the wall, and that shopkeepers magic up their goods behind the scenes! Needless to say, as children grow older, so their understanding increases in its sophistication. This social awareness is very localized, giving rise to the amazing variety of culture that we now see across the globe and indeed increasingly within most countries.

This whole area of social development is huge, and somewhat stunning to think about. We've barely scratched the surface here. I hope that this chapter has given you food for thought, and enabled you to challenge some of the givens for your group and society.

Questions for discussion

1 Which groups do you belong to? How important are they to you? Can you imagine life alone?

2 Have you been aware of 'groupthink' operating at a group that you belong to? Was that a good or bad experience?

3 How would you like to shift the thinking within your church? How could you try to achieve that shift?

4 Are you aware of judging people by their speech? Are there any accents that you find unpleasant? Can you work out why?

5 How can you help to socialize the children in church more effectively, without repressing them?

5

Faith, and how it grows

————•◆•————

*I don't know what God looks like but I know that he is powerfall
[sic] and wise.*

(Elspeth, 8)

If you were to sit in a group of people and ask what they thought
the word 'faith' means, you'd probably have as many meanings of the word as folk in the room. My thesaurus has the
following:

> Confidence, trust, reliance, assurance, conviction.
> Belief, devotion, loyalty, faithfulness, commitment, dedication.

Your group would probably have meanings with religious over-
tones, as do many of those above.

If you followed up that question with one on the role of the
Church, and by implication your children's work, then 'faith'
would probably reckon in the answers to that second question.
Helping people to find faith, to grow their faith, to have faith
develop, are all part of the agenda at most churches.

Over the last 50 years, academics have been working at the
concept of 'faith' and trying to make schemes of how faith grows
in human beings. There are recognized names in the field, and
I would like to look at the work of two of them, James Fowler
and John Westerhoff. Both have worked and written extensively
in this field, and come up with systems that help us to understand and recognize the changes and development in the faith
that we share with those among whom we live and work. Both

recognize that their work has produced tools to give insight. Neither would claim that these schemes are perfect, and both recognize that many people do not easily 'fit' the potential boxes that the schemes give us. Both are American, but the schemes are applicable to those people within the developed world who live in what are, or were, broadly Christian societies.

The insights that these theories give will ring true in many cases; but it must always be borne in mind that these theories are not proven fact. They are tools to help us understand the processes of a person's spiritual development. It is important to note that Fowler and Westerhoff use the word 'faith' as a psychological construct in their definitions and theories rather than as a theological term, so you may find the following needs thinking about carefully, with their meaning of 'faith' high in your consciousness. It is also worth taking on board that Fowler's research work focused more on adults than on children. This may take authority away from his discussion of faith development in children, but what he has to say is nevertheless important. His concentration on adults was mainly because adults are easier to interview as they tend to be more articulate, and may have been influenced by his working at a time when children's spirituality was rarely reckoned as important.

As I have already said, faith is hard to define. I sometimes say it is a slippery concept, wide and inclusive. You might like to think of it like a shawl – something that we wrap round our shoulders to keep us warm and fight off the cold. But that speaks more of a property of faith than of what it actually is – back to the top of the chapter here!

But, to give faith this clear function, that of protector, warmth, a covering that we own, is very emotive and hints at how personal faith is understood by the modern western person. So faith, in Fowler's terms, is an internal concept to which we attach great importance in our understanding of who we are as individuals. He states that all people have faith, although it may not be religious; he speaks of faith as a recognition that there is more to life than just the physical, and while that may involve belief in the transcendent, this may not be what you or I would name as 'God'. If it involves trust and a loyalty towards that transcendent being so that we develop religious faith, then we will indeed speak of 'God' and having faith in that God.

You may be thinking, 'So what's the difference between faith and spirituality?' and that is a good question. For me, faith is less emotive or intuitive and more conscious, something that you tease at mentally, working at it as a personal philosophy of life. Spirituality includes our deepest emotions – love, joy, grief – as well as how we relate to each other, which is, in my experience, rarely rational! Perhaps faith is a verb, an action, while spirituality is an experience of an inner life.

Fowler's assertion that all people have faith is widely held among people working in the fields of faith development or spirituality. You will remember the comments in Chapter 1 regarding Alister Hardy's work in the area of spirituality and religious experience, indicating that religious experience has survival value to the individual; this is now regarded with regard as trailblazing for our generation and that which preceded us. He did not refer to faith but to a form of awareness, which is not the same as the everyday normal awareness found in all human beings, which he believed to be advantageous in helping human beings to survive. He described this awareness as 'potential', implying that while it was there for all human beings, not all of us actually recognized or developed this awareness.

Westerhoff says that faith is the internal, dynamic belief while religion is the expression of that belief, and that there is a clear differential between the two. He continues that faith is deeply personal, a living, growing belief: Westerhoff would say that my religion is how I express my belief held within.

The only definition in the Bible for the word 'faith' is speaking of confidence and trust in the love of God, his power and his action in the world:

the assurance of things hoped for, the conviction of things not
seen.   (Hebrews 11.1)

It is presumed that we learn our faith through religious education, but it is possible to know all about God but not to know
God. It is equally true that one can teach adults and children
alike about the Christian religion, but one cannot give them
faith. Jesus recognized this problem when he told the parable
of the Sower, found in Mark 4.3ff. The story is told, the seeds
are sown, but only some grow, and then some that did grow die
(something we are well acquainted with in Christian education).
Within the story is the hint that something deeply mystical needs
to take place within the person to integrate the story so that
it helps faith to develop. Our task is to sow the seed and wait
for the seed to grow: the image of faith growing up with the
person. So let's examine how the faith development theories
inform our understanding of internal processes as a story is
received and taken on board, internalized, to become part of
ourselves and our own spirituality.

Fowler's stages of faith[1]

Stage 0: Undifferentiated faith

Fowler has a Stage 0 which he calls 'undifferentiated faith'.
During this period of a child's life, the seeds of faith are laid
in the form of trust, hope and love, as incoming care answers
a child's need to be cared for and loved. Children who are not
given enough one-to-one attention at this time will be severely
damaged as individuals, less able to love in a real relationship
than those whose significant others – usually parents – have met
their needs for touch, contact and love. We cannot know about
the faith of such a child as there is no way that we can access
his memories, but we can see the qualities that come from a
good experience of this stage in life: people who possess the
qualities of trust, mutuality, hope and courage will be able to

move through life in a more positive way, and their later faith development is probably more advanced. The child needs to learn a balance as to where he is in the scheme of things – to give and take in relationships – and the foundation for this quality is laid down at this stage in life. The transition to the next stage begins when thought and language begin to converge, so enabling the child to think using speech and ritualized play.

Stage 1: Intuitive-projective faith – the impulse self[2]

Children at the transition to Stage 1 will begin to play more games where they are checking out the permanence of objects; they enjoy repeatedly naming things. The shared language with others means the quality of relationship changes, and small children explore the language-based world enthusiastically. The 'what' and 'why' questions come thick and fast, and the parents may feel it will never end. The child's ability to seemingly lose interest in your answer is hard to cope with sometimes, and the interest switches immediately to something completely different but equally important (to the child). At this stage a child's thinking is not reversible, so they are working to a different logic from their long-suffering parents; we may not be able to answer their questions appropriately because the child really does have a different agenda functioning. Critically, the child has no understanding of cause and effect. 'If I do this, then that will happen,' is not going on in the child's mind. Once a person has that cause and effect, we cannot think without it coming into play. Hence the difficulty of comprehension, quite apart from the child's inevitably more limited vocabulary and thinking skills.

Stage 1 children have a relatively uncontrolled imagination, where reality and fantasy blend easily. Life is episodic, one thing after another, and is very much a montage of events which do not have a consistent narrative. Good is good and bad is bad, and the child cannot reason as an adult might. The symbols and rituals of life are deeply significant; for a child in this stage they are literally what they stand for, as the child cannot discriminate as an adult might. Children learn at an amazing rate at this stage; the brain grows and develops very rapidly. The child, however, cannot discriminate between reality and fantasy as an adult does and the two exist side by side. Faith is very much an imitation of what the child experiences from adults. Images and symbols are very important to aid understanding. While children in this stage may find the language of rituals in church difficult, images found in churches, such as stained glass windows and other symbols, will feed their spirit. Stories increasingly capture the attention of the Stage 1 child, with illustrations reinforcing the sense of the words. Many children in this stage will have a preferred book, which they will listen to and attend to repeatedly.

It is worth recognizing that even children from atheist homes have a clear, albeit very personal, concept of God. We each arrive at school with a clear understanding of what the word 'God' means, even if our environment denies God's existence.[3]

Our task in church is to provide children with a supportive environment, in which we listen to the stories and fantasies that the child brings, not telling her what to think, but giving value to her through our very being and the way that we interact with her.

Fairy tales hold tremendous importance for the child at this stage, helping him to work through all sorts of scenarios, many of which will never occur in his life, but helping him to think about the 'what-ifs' of life. Bible stories such as Daniel in the Lions' Den, and many of Jesus' parables, will be very important to children of this age, even if they don't understand them in the way that an adult will. Many of the child's positive and negative feelings will stay with her for the rest of her life, sometimes at an unconscious level, so it is important that the language we use regarding God and faith are not the negative, judgmental words to which our parents may have been subjected.

The transition to Stage 2 begins as 'concrete operations' (see Chapter 2) begin to emerge. The child is now concerned to discover what is real and what only seems to be. Bye bye, Father Christmas!

Stage 2: Mythic-literal faith – the imperial self

Children at this stage, usually aged from about 6 to about 12, have moved on to thinking skills that are based around language as well as an increasing sophistication of emotional language. The chaos of the previous stage is falling into place, with cause and effect being understood. The child now recognizes story and reality. Thought is reversible and other perspectives can be taken on board, so his own narratives will change radically, but he still cannot step back from his story and question it.

It is at this stage that telling our Christian story and stories becomes increasingly important. For Stage 2 worshippers, story is one of the key ways of understanding meaning. As we work with children of this age, the potency of story and narrative is a key constituent for supporting a child's developing faith. The child will ask, 'But is this real?' in response to stories such as the Valley of Dry Bones (Ezekiel 37). (My response to that question was that it was like Ezekiel's dream.) They like their stories to have a 'goody' and a 'baddy', so stories such as David and Goliath, or the *Star Wars* films, will be hugely popular.

Children at this stage know that God is in charge of the world and loves each one of us. A child when asked about God may actually come up with the 'old man with a beard' answer; Ruby, who is 8, drew a picture of a Love Heart in reply to what God looks like for her. God is very much like a super version of a parent, but that will be affected by the home that the child comes from.

Children at this stage cannot reflect in an abstract way, so teachers may wish to note that we cannot draw out the moral at the end of a story or parable for the children! You might like to just end a story by letting the children think about it as they go about their lives; while this is not 'giving them the gospel', it is trusting God's Spirit, and the power of the story itself, to communicate more deeply, and in the way that the child may need to hear today.

We need to realize that some adults never move past this stage. For those who do move on, puberty is the catalyst for transition.

Stage 3: Synthetic-conventional faith

This begins to be observable as the child moves into teenage years, with the accompanying self-consciousness and need to establish identity. It is accompanied by 'formal operations' (see Chapter 2) in the cognitive skills. The growing child's experiences of the world expand rapidly with the change in schooling and the way that relationships work for the individual. Faith at this stage has to work to provide the basis for the outlook and identity of the young person.

This stage is actually where many adults rest for the remainder of their life; it is one of 'conformity', of belonging to the group without questioning. The person is tuned in to the expectations and judgments of the group, and is not confident enough of his or her own identity to question profoundly and so stand aside of the group. Beliefs and values are deeply felt, but they are not beliefs and values that the person has examined critically while taking them on. Authority is located in people who are perceived to be the incumbents of the tradition, in many churches the vicar, rector or minister.

The person takes on his or her own story, and holds the past in tension with an expected future.

The problems in this stage are probably occurring to you as you read; people may give up their own judgment to the authority figure, never questioning their faith and so not being able to move into the next transition. If that authority figure is perceived to have failed them, they may despair of faith and lose religious faith altogether.

Transition to the next stage is indicated by the person (now a young adult) clashing with the tradition of the group. Policies of the group which the person regards as sacrosanct may be changed (for example, change in service from Latin to vernacular for Roman Catholics, Book of Common Prayer to *Common Worship* for Anglicans, the issue of gay marriage – the list is probably endless), provoking circumstances that challenge the belief system. Most people move into transition as they leave home and the security and support that home offers. This move from security into a more challenging world enables the young adult to question faith that may not have been developing for some time.[4]

Fowler himself points out that to move from Stage 3 onwards requires a certain level of education and articulation. If a person only achieves a minimal level of education, he will not achieve Piaget's formal operations (see Chapter 2) and will not be able to move beyond Stage 3 faith. Stage 4 requires the ability to think in the abstract, to reason and use logic. This again underlines the importance of our use of language to encourage children to widen their understanding and vocabulary and work towards formal operations.

Fowler states that for faith to grow and develop, we have to let go of our previous images and go through a short – or sometimes not so short – period of doubt and questioning. An image I find useful is that of a jigsaw puzzle. When it is completed, you see the image clearly. However, when you reach a transition period in faith development, someone has thrown your jigsaw up in the air and it has come down in lots of pieces. As you progress through the transition, the puzzle pieces are reassembled, but when you finish the transition, arriving at the next stage, you discover that, actually, the image on the puzzle has changed slightly, or even quite substantively.

Alongside Fowler's theory of faith development, we need to be aware of that developed later on by John Westerhoff.[5] Westerhoff recognizes Fowler's work but has devised his own system of faith development, which is quite different. He says faith is an action, a verb. It results from our actions with others, changing and expanding through this interaction, and it expresses itself through such actions. So Westerhoff places faith entirely within a community of faith – it is not possible to be a person of faith who lives in isolation. Westerhoff speaks of faith with a religious subtext, whereas Fowler believes people of no religious persuasion, as well as those who have religious persuasion, may have faith.

Westerhoff's theory of faith development

Westerhoff sees faith very much along the lines of a tree, growing and spreading, where the development of faith is the equivalent of the rings found inside the bark. He proposes four styles of faith rather than stages, and each grows around the previous style or ring. Therefore the person who has moved right through faith, and has moved to the fourth style, contains within himself the previous three, and needs to attend to the needs of all four styles of faith. Indeed, if the needs of a 'previous', deeper buried style of faith are not being met, the person will defer back to the earlier style and meet the needs of that style before returning to the more recent style of faith.

This is a clear difference with Fowler, who proposes that a person 'leaves' each stage as she moves through life. Westerhoff also insists that there is no 'pecking order' of faith: no style is in any way 'superior' or 'better' than any other. It's simply where you are at the present time. Fowler clearly sees the later stages of faith as movement and progress, rather as a PhD is further than a BA, as A levels are further than GCSEs. So he sees life as a progress towards Stage 6. Westerhoff has a more egalitarian feel to his theory.

Westerhoff believes that faith will only grow if given the right environment; it is possible to arrest faith development by not giving the right conditions for growth, just as trees will stop growing if there is a drought, they become pot-bound or the soil does not contain the right nutrients. He points out that this is still a complete tree; it's just not growing or developing any more. So he says we need interaction with other people of faith if we are to grow and develop. Faith is an action that includes thinking, feeling and willing. It is transmitted, sustained and expanded through our interactions with other people of faith in community. These interactions are the nutrients and water that keep the tree of faith growing and developing.

Trees grow slowly – very slowly in most cases – so we don't notice them growing, and faith is like this. We may suddenly notice a change, just as my children always seemed to grow overnight and I only noticed the growth as we said our 'Goodbye' in the morning and stood next to each other. So we don't see the growth in faith slowly taking place, but we will notice the result. Growth like this cannot be forced or rushed; we can just be with people as they slowly move from one style of faith, making the new ring as they take on a new style of faith.

Style 1: Experienced faith

This results from interactions with others of faith. No one can determine another's faith or give someone faith, but we share our lives and faith with one another. Others do the same, and through this mutual giving and receiving we sustain and transmit and expand our faith. This is the style of faith of the preschool and early childhood years, where faith is experienced through action and interaction. All children initiate action and respond to the actions of others; they will explore and test, imagine and create, experience and react in their day-to-day lives. This is how they learn, from putting food into their mouths to find out if they like it, and find it's good, to responding to the love and care of their parents and carers. Children's actions influence those with whom they interact – a laugh or a disgruntled noise will elicit very different responses. The actions of others will affect and influence them. Their acts prove a mirror and test for those they interact with. We all recognize the scenario where children push things to the limit to discover where the boundaries are, or where they need to draw out precisely what the ground rules are; children can live with different rules in different places easily and with no seeming effort once the rules have been explained. So they take off their shoes as they enter one friend's house, while at another they walk mud all over the new cream carpet!

The characteristics of this type of faith continue for us all and are foundational to all people's faith. For example, we all need to be hugged: it is easy with children but more difficult with teenagers or adults. We all need to continue to act in ways that explore and test, imagine and create, experience and react. We continue to learn as we meet new people, develop new relationships and engage in new patterns of working and being.

For all people, experiences relating to words are more important than the words themselves. You say you love me – OK, but I'll expect you to act in that way too or I'll soon think I can't take you at your word. Our language and experience are interrelated to the point where we find it difficult to think of one without the other; we think about our experiences in language, after all. The three most important experiences are trust, love and acceptance for Christians and this need continues throughout life. We should be 'doers of the word, and not merely hearers' (James 1.22). People who do not act as Christians are soon recognized by those outside the community of faith, who will quickly level the accusation of hypocrisy.

Thus, for this style of faith to flourish, we need to provide an environment of sharing and interaction between people of faith. We all need to be Christian with others, all of the time.

Style 2: Affiliative faith

If experienced faith can be modelled as two people looking up and down, or as a child holding an adult's hand, this style of faith is much more egalitarian, like two people facing each other, or two people of the same age holding hands, walking side by side. It comes after successful experienced faith, and builds upon that style. Style 2 is all about acting with others in an accepting community with a clear sense of identity. We all need to belong to a self-conscious community, able to actively participate and share in its life, and in a church community this is often seen through people joining the choir or the youth club, or acting as sidespeople or stewards at worship services. We all have a need to feel wanted and needed, to be missed when we're not there, and to contribute to the whole.

This is a period of religious affections and heartfelt belief. A person's intuitional way of being there is as important as the intellectual; I need to feel my faith as much as I think about my faith. So you see people participating in the arts – drama, music, dance, painting and so forth – and this involvement is critical for working out the emotional attachment to the faith as well as Bible reading reflecting the thinking-through of faith.

Authority is found in the community's communication of a story and way of life that judges and inspires actions. So the teaching of the faith through formal situations is primal for the person in this style of faith.

Style 2 faith is first experienced through action, then experienced through images and story. Thus there is the need to learn the community's story, and to internalize, rehearse and personally own the story that undergirds the community's faith. This again is done through the formal teaching of the community: Sunday school or sermon, Bible class or youth club quiet times.

Typically, this is the faith of young teenagers, as they begin to take on the responsible roles of the community, and so become integrated into adult membership of the group.[6]

The children we work with within the scope of the church's mission are all found somewhere on the continuum described by Fowler and Westerhoff above. There will be some children that Fowler's scheme seems to describe better than Westerhoff's, and there will be others for whom Westerhoff seems to have the fit far more accurately. Both schemes are simply tools to help us to understand what is going on as we all develop and grow in our faith as human beings. For us as children's workers, the crux is to be able to stand alongside our children as they grow and develop, to nurture and encourage them as they grow in their own faith towards the integrity of person that faith offers. If understanding these theories of how they are growing enables me to be there more fully for the children with whom I have been entrusted, then it is worth the reading and thinking.

Questions for discussion

1 Think about a child whom you find perplexing. How does having some insight into faith development theory help you to work alongside this child?
2 You might like to read more about this area, and so think through where you are in Fowler's stages.
3 Do you recognize your faith in any of Fowler's stages? Do you think you need to move on, or are you content with your faith as it is?
4 How much do you encourage children to ask the difficult questions that accompany moving on in faith?

6

An overview

*Amy (5) looked up at the bright shining sun. 'Hello, Grandad,'
she said.*

You've probably worked your way through the first few
chapters of this book wondering just how all these different
theories apply to you as you teach the children week by week.

What we need to do now is to stick them all together, to
overlay the differing theories to see what they can tell us about
children at different stages of development. This should give
us a way in to understand the different, and sometimes very
strange, behaviours that we see in our children.

Early childhood

Let's begin where we begin in church, with children who are
in what we could call 'early childhood': children from about 2
to 6 years old. Younger children are not usually in a special group
in a church context, other than a crèche, and there we encourage healthy play and activity, using the many toys available (and
usually donated in this context!).

Children from about 2 years upwards are in the stage that
Piaget called 'preoperational' or 'intuitive'. These are children
who are brimming with imagination and creativity. They see
the world very much from their own perspective, and cannot
see it from another's point of view. These are the children who
don't understand conservation – remember the thing about juice

glasses? They are still learning how to behave in a social setting, so our children will, from time to time, get it seriously wrong, and we need to support and encourage them as they learn socialization skills. Our local schools have the 'carpet' area in their classrooms, and children respond well to that defined area, learning to sit quietly in that area, listening to whoever is speaking and indicating by putting up their hand, or some other technique, that they wish to contribute to the discussion. (One class throws a small cuddly dog to the child who can speak, always via the teacher. Try it – it works well with 5- to 7-year-olds: 'You can only speak if you're holding Patch or Rover or Bouncer the dog . . .')

Children of this age will mirror other children's behaviour. If one child laughs out loud, chances are that the others will too, sometimes making a horrible forced laugh sound as they join in with a joke they may not have understood in their attempt to be part of the larger group. Children coming into this stage will still throw tantrums (so do some adults, but that's another subject) but as they move through this stage they come to realize, especially if they are well handled, that they cannot always have their own way. More importantly, they come to realize that there is more than one way, and begin to be able to take that on board.

From Erikson's point of view, there are two stages during this period. First comes 'autonomy versus shame', a period of increasing independence from the child's carer; toilet training and other forms of independence, such as learning how to eat with cutlery, are still going on, and how far the child has progressed will depend on his motor skills – and these are incredibly variable. Using a knife and fork is a very complicated skill, but to those of us who do it all the time . . . It is very important that we are supportive of children as they tackle these skills. Watching children colour, or do a jigsaw and other hand-to-eye co-ordinated tasks, shows us how different children of this age can be, and gives a pretty good indication of how manually dextrous the child will be when grown up. Even doing up shoes with Velcro fasteners is a challenge for some children of this age. Don't assume!

Once the child has reached about 4 to 5 years, she will enter the stage called 'initiative versus guilt'. You will see this as the child begins to organize games: rules and regulations become more important. Friendships become mutual. Learning is accelerating as the child 'mops up' whatever she can.

In Fowler's scheme of faith development, the child will be in the stage he calls 'intuitive-projective faith – the impulse self'. As the child explores language, laying down the enormous bank of words that stand for various concepts, he will chatter and query, sometimes non-stop. It's important for us to remember that this child does not have reversible thinking – he really can't flip ideas around as adults do, so we need to keep our expectations realistic The child lives in a world where one thing follows another; it's a straight line, and there is no understanding of the subtle shades of grey that adults use when reasoning. Someone is either a 'goody' or a 'baddy', but we understand that sometimes something fantastic takes place and the baddy becomes good. Symbols and rituals are very important, so don't forget to sing 'Happy Birthday' or do a proper Nativity play! Some children of this age will love to look in church buildings at the significant pieces of architecture, as they cement a child's present understanding of faith. Children at this age do not have their own concept of faith, but have acquired a kind of second-hand version from the adults with whom they share their lives. At this point, it is very important to allow space for the child to take in the rites and rituals of church. She may not understand, but that understanding will develop and grow. Story becomes increasingly important at this time; both secular and sacred stories will take up a lot of time – watch children acting out their favourite stories in the playground, and at church. The Old Testament in particular will score highly, with baddies such as Goliath, and goodies such as David feeding the child's imagination and understanding.

Westerhoff places children's faith right through to adolescence as 'experienced faith'. A child's faith at this stage is a reflection of the faith that he experiences from other people; through a child's experimentation and interaction with the world, he will develop and grow in his faith. If adults are kind, patient and accepting of the child, then he will associate this with church, faith and being a Christian; I don't need to spell out the corollary. Children see people's reactions to them as a mirror of themselves, and they need to have rules and boundaries clearly defined and adhered to in church as well as at home. Westerhoff's model requires people to be clearly Christian in every area of their lives if our children are to grow and develop in faith.

At this stage a child is highly susceptible to our view of God, so we need to ensure that what we teach about God is reflecting a biblical, loving perspective and is not overlaid with our own personal hang-ups. In my daily work, I come across people who in their deep beliefs have a very fierce model of God. This is often communicated by their worrying about a deceased loved one, and 'where they are now'. People with this view of a judgmental God frequently fear that, because the person was not a confessing Christian, they have not gone to heaven. Such worriers tend to be older, coming from a generation that heard sermons about hell and damnation rather more than my own flock do at present, and this model of God is deeply imprinted within their psyche, giving a God who is demanding and people who are fearful of committing mortal sin every time they do anything tending towards the fun or risky or dubious. This is the generation that will be grandparents and great-grandparents, and these are often the people who are the practising Christians in today's society. The example that the children receive from the adults at church is therefore very important, and we need to be always aware of the model of God that we have uppermost within our own understanding. Using a good scheme will help here, as it will give guidelines as to how to interact with the children and the day's lesson most effectively for all.

Be aware that children who suffer abuse of any type will have a damaged model of what a parent is like. Sadly, it's frequently fathers who come out worst here, so do try to have both male and female adults with your class, and be conscious of the modelling that is going on through the way that adults interact with each other, so that damaged children come to see that there is a different way of relating – one that is more like our Heavenly Father.

Mid and late childhood

From about 6, children move on for all three models. Piaget calls his next stage 'concrete operations'. Logical thinking is beginning to occur, reading is enabling children to feed their imaginations through their own choice of materials and resources, and they have developed the ability to take a concrete object and draw a generalization from it. So, for example, we can group some stories and call them 'parables'. Bible stories are enjoyed more and more, and children of this age will enjoy learning facts and figures so it's good to use these in our teaching.

Erikson's name for this stage is 'industry versus inferiority'. This is the stage where children absorb the cultural norms of their society, so worship and interior life need to be reflected by the home. Children at this stage like to make things, so encourage this in the children in your care – think of all those worksheets that the Sunday school schemes provide! Let them make their own Christingles and Easter Gardens, let them paint and engage with lots of different craft activities. This is the age at which they love to share 'what we've been doing' with the adult congregation, holding up whatever they've made this week to show. As the name implies, they continue to need positive reinforcement, carrots rather than sticks, in their lives. At present, the morality of the reality TV show is prevalent in many children's lives, and this often comes with quite appalling treatment of people being seen as normal. Again, modelling 'Christ-like' attitudes, questioning these norms and being Christ-like to the children will help them to question the values of the society around us. This is, of course, laying enormous responsibility at the feet of the adults who care for our children, and this should be acknowledged and honoured within the church. Ensuring that the carrots are non-material is also important in this time of cash-rich time-poor parents. These children are bought off all too often; quality time is always the best reward we can give them.

In Fowler's scheme, we now come to 'mythic-literal faith – the imperial self'. This can be a tricky stage to work with children, as they will begin to question, 'But is it real, is it true?' They haven't as yet the sophisticated thinking processes that allow them to understand 'what is truth' and complex thinking around literal and metaphorical truth, but we need to be there to help them to work on it. Story is critical for children at this stage, as they work on their own part in the faith story in which they share. Their thinking is reversible and they can begin to understand someone else's point of view, so they will ask increasingly sophisticated questions. We need to remember their inability to take a moral from a story; teachers at day school in particular will be used to telling the children 'what the story means today', but I suggest you stop! Simply tell the story, and then ask the children to think about it during the day and see what they think it's all about. It's a bit scary as a learning technique, as we then trust the child and the Holy Spirit to work together towards what the story really said to that child today – and that may be quite incomprehensible to us as adults! Stage 2 'faith-ers' like to be given rules and regulations, to know their boundaries and what is right and what is wrong. It is during the next stage that the big questions will be asked!

The main thing to remember with all these levels is that the children do not have the power of abstract thinking. (Neither do some adults.) So we need to keep our lessons concrete-based, using lots of visual materials, and allowing the child to rework the story afterwards.

Adolescence

So we come to the big one – adolescence! This stage begins once a child starts to become self-conscious and self-aware in a new way. You know what I mean! However, and this is very important, if a child has built up a real and good working relationship with the adults she meets in church, we can be very important to her as she becomes a young person and is inevitably in conflict with her parents or carers from time to time.

Piaget defines this stage as 'formal operations', and this stage continues into adulthood. The key point is the beginning of abstract thought and the self-consciousness that brings a developing young adult a whole new way of relating. Peer groups become very important, and if young people are moving in a group outside of Christianity and the Church it becomes increasingly hard for them to stay with us at this time. One of our older boy choristers was recently caught seriously on the back foot when one of his (male) school friends appeared in the congregation. By the time we got to the end of the service he'd come up with the ultimate reason for being in a church choir: 'Just look at all those girls!' he declared to his suddenly very envious friend. There are indeed three girls to every boy!

Erikson names this phase 'Identity versus role confusion' and this sums up a great deal of how those of us for whom this stage was way back in the mists of time see adolescence! We should never underestimate how hard this stage can be as our young people develop their own personalities and decide who they really are as opposed to who their family or carers wish them to be. We all know about door-slamming, summed up brilliantly in the Harry Enfield character 'Kevin'. Indeed, my husband and I sometimes called our own teenagers 'Kevin' when they were a bit out of line (as if!) and it worked very well. Using the language of topical comedy characters helps our young people to know that we have some awareness of their world, although we oldies have to guard against being too trendy – there is a need to break away, and for us to recognize we aren't the same age, and we don't have the same pressures. At the time of writing, *Little Britain* is just past its peak and I'm waiting for the next big thing.

For us in church, this is a very threatening stage, as children leave church rapidly at this stage, or they grasp their childish faith hard and hold tight to it as if it's a protection against the storm that they are living through.

Fowler calls this stage of faith 'synthetic-conventional faith'. Faith at this stage has to work to provide the basis for the outlook and identity of the young person. Adolescents are well tuned in to conformity at this point, and they will trim their thinking sometimes to fit in with what they experience around them. They need to feel that they are part of a larger group, so Sunday schools who have a group for young teenagers will now call it by a different name, such as 'Pathfinders'; chances are it will have a more youth-club feel, perhaps with an evening meeting. Relationships between the young people are incredibly important, and rows can be vicious and stormy but brief and quickly overcome. The authority figure for these young people is critical. They may well absolutely believe them, which is scary for you if you are cast in this role. The young person may stay in this stage possibly for the rest of his life, moving through adulthood by not attending to the questions that occur or by belonging to a church that is more authoritarian in its style.

There may come a point where the young person, usually about 18 by now, begins to ask questions of her assumed faith to which, as far as she can see, the only answer is outside of

Christian faith. This usually comes with the big move away from home, especially if they go to university, out of the real sphere of influence of their parents or carers.[1] It is vital that the adults stay in touch with these young people, affirming them as they struggle with their faith as they move through Stage 4, so that they arrive at the position of a faith that is open to question and their own, owned faith. Many people are lost to the Church at this time, but they are frequently the ones who come back once they are parents themselves, so don't despair. My own feeling is that it's more important for our young people to leave the Church and struggle to find their own faith than to stay in the Church with a childish faith that is not robust and able to dialogue with the world in which they move.

According to Westerhoff, if a child has a successful history of experienced faith, then as he enters adolescence, his faith will move into the 'affiliative faith style'. This is about belonging, with the importance already seen of peer groups, helping in church with various tasks, being seen to be a real member. If we are feeling brave enough to look at these children as they move towards adulthood, the health of their faith will give us an idea of how we have been communicating our faith and sharing with them. As the child's emotional life becomes more reflective, the opportunity to join in with drama, music and the arts around church enables her to 'feel' her faith as well as thinking it. This is particularly important and quite challenging for people whose personality is more intellectually than intuitively based. Children need to learn the story of their own faith and the story of this particular community of faith, so times spent together reflecting on the shared journey will be of benefit to all. It is during adolescence that we see personality traits firming up, as the introverts and extroverts become more so and learning styles become more obvious. Personality is never set, but the stronger, dominant traits are becoming more accentuated at this time.

How do we respond to these changes and needs within the church?

First, it is important that the needs of children at different stages are catered for, and this means that the model you use needs to be fluid as children of different stages and ages pass through your group. Inevitably, many Sunday school teachers are there because their children are learners. This is great, as it often means the parents are learning about the Christian faith alongside their children, and they are also well aware of what their children can and cannot manage. The problem comes if they forget what their children were like as they grow older, and the group can become targeted towards a very defined group of children and their particular needs. So you do need ideally to have someone there who does not have that tie to a particular child or group.

The Key Stage 1 (Infants) Key Stage 2 (Juniors) division used by day schools may have been arrived at accidentally, but as we've seen, there is sense in breaking the group at about 6 years, as faith, cognitive and personality development all go through a change at this point. Clearly, after adolescence hits, you will need to radically change the provision for any children who are still with you. They may join the team as 'junior leaders', or they may choose to go and sit in with the adults. Children who joined the church choir at about 7 and who wish to leave it (boys especially, as their voices break) may find it very hard to sit with the rest of the congregation, so consider a special role for these young people; we try to recruit them as servers, but that's very Anglican–RC.

The various schemes and materials that are on the market vary enormously, and you will have found the scheme that suits your church, but I would encourage you to look at the chapter on Godly Play and think about incorporating different story-telling styles in your group. Buy more schemes than the one you habitually use and cannibalize the best bits into your regular scheme – variety is the spice of life.

Consider how you begin your week-by-week sessions: do you have a quiet start or a noisier one? When I started in my present post, we had a stunningly talented young man who started the week's session with dancing, doing actions to Christian songs in a way that I had never seen before. (Or since.) The children adored this young man (who is now a professional puppeteer) and would hurtle in through the doors! They then had a quiet 'down' time incorporated into the session so that everyone could get their breath back. After this young man left us for gainful employment (and how we missed him!) we developed a quiet colouring time during the children's arrival. This has now become singing songs to a newer teacher's guitar-playing. So use what you've got, and aim for a start that uses the talents you have and the children who are attending. Both the dancing and the singing starts suit more extrovert children better than the more sensitive, shy children. As we encourage parents to stay with their children for the first few sessions, we rely on the parents to help their children join this noisier activity, or to look at the books that are always available in the quiet corner of the room.

As you move into the story time, let all your teachers tell the story. Everyone will have a different style, and variety is good. Variety in your response time, be it doing drama, crafts or other responses, is critical. Children like to know the structure and what will happen within a broad-brush outline, but will become bored if every week is effectively the same.

Never forget the importance of language: language and vocabulary are the building bricks of children's understanding of God, their faith and their spirituality. Without the vocabulary the children cannot understand. So ensure that your story-telling uses the right words. Children are used to jargon and technical language. I recently entered a Year 5 class (9–10) and they were learning about metaphors and similes. I still can't remember which is which, but we expect our children to, and many do. So don't underestimate the blotting-paper nature of a child's ability to learn new, correct words and use them.

I would encourage you to increasingly involve all young people in the tasks of church, perhaps convening a junior PCC or church committee, so that they have a chance to speak and be heard.[2] Use them as stewards or sidespeople. They are often better readers than all those adults who dominate the reading rota. Why can't they lead the prayers? How about taking the collection? The more they are used for perceived adult roles, the more they will feel that we are taking them seriously as committed members of the church. And don't forget that the older children may be listening to sermons now: let them have a chance to discuss them with the preacher. They often have far more questions than the adults in the congregation, who aren't usually working out their own faith with anything like the same commitment or drive. Plan well together, socialize together and enjoy each other's contributions.

Most Sunday school groups have a named leader and it is important that that role is time-defined. After a few years, this person may well want a rest, even if that rest is becoming one of the regular helpers (as long as they don't try to take that authority back).

Questions for discussion

1 How challenging do you find this consideration of different areas of child development? Have you considered these areas before?
2 How does your group need to adjust its working to include the awareness of children's different development?
3 What represents the biggest challenge to you personally in this chapter?

7

Godly Play

———◦•◦———

We were attending a very high church, where the priest held a piece of the consecrated bread in his fingers as he blessed children on the head. When we got back to our pew, Jim turned and said, 'You got yours in your mouth, but I got mine through my head.'

In this chapter I want to briefly examine the system of Christian education called 'Godly Play' through an overview of its development and a description of how a Godly Play session is run.

Open and closed learning

The English educational system works in a rather measured way. Children are tested and ability is measured as they progress from nursery through to graduation. The emphasis in school over the last decade or so has become very much a question of learning concepts, and being able to prove that the child has done so. Few people question the actual process of learning going on in our schools, and even those who do tend to concentrate on the mind, leaving the spiritual to those they regard as better qualified.

The Christian education of children has followed the secular trend; success for a Sunday school teacher may be a verbal discussion to demonstrate how much of the story the children can remember and what it means. Most Sunday teaching materials guide teachers towards the telling of the story, some interactive recall of the story, craftwork, and possibly a worksheet, with the child being guided clearly along the pattern for the session. This is good for both teachers and students in that it gives security and given outcomes, and mimics the system that the child will know from school, but it may limit children from questioning and wondering about issues that the story has aroused for them. It is described as a closed system of learning; it follows a clear path, from beginning to end, and 'sidetracking' from children can be regarded as interruption rather than a real request to let the process develop in a new direction.

The process we experience in much Christian education has been described, rather negatively, as 'sacred baby-sitting', and many adults in our churches want exactly that – for the children to be outside of the 'main' worship, being kept busy and learning the Christian faith. And the quieter the better![1]

Open and closed questions

Much of the teaching in school is in the form of questions and answers. Teachers do this because it keeps the children concentrating, and helps them to check whether the children are keeping up with the flow of information and subject matter as the lesson proceeds. If the teacher senses a child's attention wandering, he can bring it back by a question to check whether that child is 'with us'. If the questions can be answered with a 'yes' or 'no', or a very brief answer, then that question is defined as closed. So, in maths, if I asked, 'What's two plus two?' there is only one answer that is correct. Likewise, in science I may ask a child what the thermometer is reading as water boils, and the answer will be in the region of 100 degrees. Closed questions tend to be right or wrong, and are usually to do with learning information – facts.

If I asked a child a question about a poem, such as, 'What do you think the person is feeling at this point?' the child could say all sorts of things, and each would be right. The child could say a few words or quite a few, and again, either is right. This is an open question, which is asking someone to be expansive, to elucidate their personal feelings or beliefs, and has no right or wrong answer. Open questions tend to be used to get children to express their own ideas. Open questions are designed to open up a child's thinking rather than funnel it into a particular way of thinking or a particular piece of knowledge.

Both types of question have their uses, but in religious education we want to be using more open questions than closed: we want to enable children to work at their own spirituality rather than give them a watered-down version of our own.

The process of Christian education

Christian educators easily fall into the trap of equating knowledge with faith. We have already noticed that knowing about God is not the same as knowing God – we can teach children the Bible so that they can recite it from beginning to end without experiencing anything spiritual in that recitation. Theology graduates may describe themselves as atheist. What we are about is helping children to make sense of the world from a spiritual standpoint. Knowing the story is not the same as being part of the story – as we noted earlier, the epistle of James says, 'Be doers of the word, and not merely hearers' (James 1.22). But who decides what a story means? How does the listener hear the story and process it in such a way that the story is internalized, that it enters his very being, his make-up as a person, and is recognized as part of his life, his own story? Preachers and teachers tell the story and expand it, but necessarily starting from the impact that the story has on them. The assumption is made that the listeners are following the story in the same way as the person teaching, but this cannot be supposed. Every listener brings a different experience of life, and every listener thinks in a different way from everyone else. The story will impact on every listener in a different way, and it would be good practice to encourage listeners and teachers alike to recognize this and then work with the story as is best for them – indeed, as the Spirit leads. This is a far more open way to approach the story.

Recognition of the superiority of this method of sharing sacred stories is reflected in the increase in the storytelling style of sermon, where the ends are left open, with the individual person, having 'arrived' in the narrative, working through it as the story speaks to them. If a person is to enter into a story there has to be an element of giving up control. She then actively lives within the story's time and space while the story is being communicated through its telling. This stirs the imagination in a more creative way, as the story will enter into the right side of the brain, where emotion and sensing take place.

Ideally the storytelling is an interpersonal telling, with the listeners responding and the teller responding in turn to the listeners. A chorus or words that repeat is an ideal way to achieve this type of telling. In the book of Daniel, in the Old Testament, there are many stories where there is a chorus line. The one I like the best is the story of the Golden Statue, leading into the story of the Fiery Furnace, found in chapter 3. King Nebuchadnezzar (don't you just love that name!) made a huge statue, and set it up for everyone to worship him, including 'the satraps, the prefects, and the governors, the counsellors, the treasurers, the justices, the magistrates, and all the officials of the provinces' (Daniel 3.2, 3). There is a musical accompaniment to the worship, and that acts as a call to worship 'the sound of the horn, pipe, lyre, trigon, harp, drum, and entire musical ensemble' (vv. 5, 7, 15).[2]

Look at the word-by-word repeats! Children – and adults – listening to this story would have all come in on these crazy repeating lists. There is little as effective in keeping people's attention in a story (or a song or hymn) as repeating choruses that we all join in.

So, we need to give our listeners the chance to participate fully and to experience open rather than closed learning, with open rather than closed questions being employed. This challenges our teaching methods, implying that there might be other ways to teach which would facilitate more open learning, and perhaps enable children to make more sense of the spiritual world in which they live.

The development of Godly Play

Through the second half of the last century, people concerned for the spiritual growth of children worked to devise a new way of telling stories and of sharing and nurturing a child's spiritual life, rather than imposing an adult model. One of the outcomes of this work is a method of storytelling and interaction with children which is called 'Godly Play'. Godly Play is concerned with religious growth and how to foster it. Jerome Berryman, in his book entitled *Godly Play* explains the method in great detail, but in a nutshell the emphasis all through this method is in helping children to understand religious language and to use it in a creative and liberating manner. Godly Play takes seriously the idea that, without appropriate language, we cannot grow in our spiritual understanding of the world, and aims to give us the language to do the work that needs to be done if adults are to understand their faith as clearly as a doctor might understand physiology. Without religious language, we cannot make sense of our spiritual nature, as we don't have the language to develop the concepts internally. Godly Play is designed to aid the use of religious language by the individual, within the context of carefully structured sessions.

The Godly Play process does not seem as structured as many Sunday school lessons, nor are the learning outcomes as explicit; this is about teaching children how to enter into the divine game of life. These structures have been carefully devised down through years of experimental research and testing to facilitate open learning. From the design of the learning environment, through the pattern of the session, scrupulous thought has gone into the total experience that the children share with their teachers.

The Godly Play session: entering

The Godly Play session is modelled on the structure of the Eucharist. The room the children come to has been designed and laid out to facilitate indirect learning.[3] The full Godly Play classroom may not be available for all – few church groups can dedicate a room for just Godly Play use – but if you do have such a room, the layout draws the children into the essence of the open style of learning and reflects all sorts of nonverbal messages for the learners, from the respect, equality and learning stance of both adults and children to physical commodities such as the materials for the lessons based around the church year with its seasons. If, like most of us, you cannot dedicate a room just for Godly Play, a trolley or set of shelves carefully used will have to suffice. The idea is that all the materials used are there, and available for each child to use should he or she so desire. Ideally, some lessons are in woven baskets, others in gold boxes, others carefully stored along the floor. The focus is on Christ in some form – perhaps a lovely hanging or tapestry. The Holy Family is there, as is a light, and the model to represent the Good Shepherd. The room is designed to give an environment that speaks to those present of God's love in Jesus.

The visual stimuli, the materials, the layout, as well as the way that the adults interact and relate to each other and the children, all work on the indirect level to teach about God and the community working together. The children are recognized as a community, the Body of Christ, just as much as the adults who are worshipping elsewhere. There is a welcoming person, the 'greeter' at the door, so that each child feels welcomed and valued as he or she arrives. Unlike many Sunday schools, the parents and carers leave their children at the door; it has been explained and agreed that the child is entering a sacred space, where their work is play. The adults might prove distracting – and, more importantly, it is the children's space. If a child is fractious or unsettled, he stays with the greeter to calm down, and so slowly enters the special space. When the child is ready to participate, he moves into a waiting circle of all the other children, with the storytelling adult already present. The story-teller greets each child. They sit, forming the circle as the children arrive. They then wait for the others, with quiet con-versation initiated by the storyteller, as they ascertain what has been going on in each participant's life. The children are encouraged to sit with their legs crossed as a way of indicating their readiness for what is about to take place. They are open-ing themselves up for learning.

Development: story

Once all are ready, the storyteller will tell the story. This is very different from much storytelling today. The story is told with the help of visual aids, often wooden models. There is no eye contact between storyteller and child; all attention is focused on the story. The narrative words have been learned as a script; and although many people struggle with this, these scripts 'work' for the children. Many years of research and analysis and experience have pared down the stories to the best form, so there is minimal personal input from the storyteller. The aim is to provide 'just the story'. This method aims to draw the children into the story, to show them how to use religious language to make meaning, and it may be that the child also encounters God through that internalization of the language, the jargon, the special, specific vocabulary of faith, as she works through the story unfolding before her eyes. Critically, it means that every time the child hears a story, the person who tells it is not import-ant for maintaining the quality and accuracy of the story. That story remains the same, enabling the child to take the words and work on them over and over again, very like an adult hearing one of Jesus' parables. We have all experienced the jolt of hearing a much loved story from a new version or translation of the Bible, when the wording changes just as you arrive at the bit that you really thought you knew by heart! In my life, the jump from 'I will make you fishers of men' to 'I will make you fish for people' was quite shocking!

The story is told slowly, the visual aids moved around the central space to reinforce the words, with plenty of pauses so that the full power of the language can be taken in. The modern need for bigger, brasher, more exciting storytelling is not present in the Godly Play context. The aim is to give the story space to speak for itself. This can feel very strange, like putting a brake on for a child in a culture where bigger and brasher is so much the order of the day.

My own experience of being part of a Godly Play session as a learner is that the story 'sucks you in'. You find stories that you've heard many times before suddenly regain their power to move and change you – it's quite extraordinary. In some way the method of storytelling seems to reclaim the imaginative power of the original teller, speaking down through the centuries in a fresh way. The other observation that I would make is that, for me, the story seems to bypass my intellect and go to my emotional intelligence, the right side of the brain, in a way that few other experiences of the same story have done in the past.

Development: wondering

At the end of the story there is a time to wonder. The storyteller cues the process with some 'I wonder' questions. These are designed to help the children internalize the story, to help them to be there, for example, as one of the sheep in the parable of the Lost Sheep.

'I wonder if the sheep have names.'

'I wonder if you've ever felt lost and heard the Good Shepherd call your name.'[4]

Most importantly, the 'I wonder' gives permission for the children to let the story take them further, to explore the feelings and thoughts that have been aroused either by articulating their thoughts or by staying with them internally. Their imagination has been within the story; it is a time to let their creative thinking flow, to encourage engagement with the language of the story. Critically, the storyteller does not have an end point in view. This is not about checking whether the children have grasped a particular concept, or understood the learning outcome of the lesson. This is one of the points where Godly Play is aiming to model truly open learning. Wondering is intended to encourage children to utilize religious language for themselves, and to understand such language when others use it. If any part of the process could be described as the most important part of the children's work of the day, it is this time of wondering, of being open and receptive.

Read the following example of a wondering session, at the end of the parable of the Good Shepherd, and try to see where the children's minds and hearts have wandered. ST stands for Story Teller; the responses come from a class of 9- to 10-year-olds in a church primary school. Note also that the storyteller gives no clues as to where she wants the conversation to go – it is driven by the children's wondering.

ST: I wonder if you've ever heard the Good Shepherd call your name.
I wonder if the sheep were happy in there –
I wonder where this might really be.
I wonder who the sheep might really be.

Child: They could be us and the Good Shepherd could be like Jesus.

ST: Is that what you think?

Child: The sheep could be angels.

ST: The sheep could be angels.

Child: The sheep could be Jesus' followers.

Child: The sheep could be Jesus and his disciples.

ST: The sheep could be Jesus' disciples.
        I wonder where the sheepfold is really, and I wonder where this (indicating the visual aid world) might really be.
        Now I wonder how listening to that story made you feel.

Child: Relaxed.

ST: Relaxed.

Child: Peaceful.

ST: Peaceful.

Child: Really calm.

ST: Really calm.

Child: It made me think.

ST: Made you think. What about?

Child: About . . . things that . . . It made me feel relaxed and it was good to watch because like . . . God like with his followers.

ST: Ah ha.

Child: . . . sheep that got lost.[5]

Godly Play acknowledges that children also have fears and doubts about the meaning of life and death. The spirituality of the children is being recognized, not as that of an adult 'watered down' in some way, but as unique and as relevant to the child as that of an adult. Thus Godly Play is taking the development of children's spiritual lives to be of fundamental, primary importance. It also recognizes that children understand their own boundary – that there is more to life than just me and my physical presence. It gives children the space to explore their relationship with the visible and the invisible world to which they are relating.

Development: responding

The group is then given a chance to respond further to the story. There is no intentional guidance as to what they should do in terms of the adults giving materials that direct the child's thinking or imagination to draw, write or create, but every child is asked to choose freely what work they would like to undertake, be it with crayons, paint, clay or play dough – whatever the child requests. Each week is not a discrete section and it may be that some return to work in progress. The storyteller will ask around the circle, and the greeter will assist each child to collect the materials needed to work on the story. The children take time to work through creative materials to explore how the story has impacted on them. This gives the story time to register and be interiorized, owned and part of the child's world. They are not told what to do, neither are they given materials that would control their creativity – it is the equivalent of a blank sheet and they can make of it what they will. It may be that a child takes out one of the boxes containing stories, or one of the other visual cues to a passage previously explored. This means she probably has unfinished business within that area, and she is encouraged to continue that work.

The responses to the storytelling can be quite startling; here is a conversation with a child, discussing the painting she produced as a response to the Good Shepherd:

L: I think the story at the moment was like, it was, it was probably like about all the . . . sheep, the sheep probably felt like really lonely when he was in the forest and then all his, all his other sheep came back and found him or maybe they, they got – had an argument or something and then they called him and they found that they really – that they couldn't live without him so they went back to get him.

ST: Lovely, that's lovely. Is there anything else that you want to say about the story?

L: I think that the sheep were far better when they were all back in the sheepfold and they were all together so they could just chat.

ST: Chat [laughter], so they could all chat – that's lovely.[6]

Note how the child had really entered the story: the sheep is acting in an incredibly childlike way in the listener's mind, 'They had an argument or something.' This understanding of the story is based right in the child's world and experience, not some far-off place called 'religion'. And they get back together to chat! The storyteller was just as amused as you are reading that!

Another example:

ST: I wonder if you could tell me how the story made you feel, the story of the Good Shepherd.

J: Well, it says in the poem, it's a story of roller-coaster emotions if you will. Em, every time the story just kept changing, all the emotions, they kept coming to me quickly.

ST: Which emotions can you remember?

J: Well, at the beginning, the beginning the Good Shepherd, well, it's all between the beginning and the end.

ST: Uh-huh.
       And you've got the emotions in the poem, haven't you? Can you read your poem, so that we can hear you reading it?

J: It made me feel like I hadn't before, all that and a whole lot more.
       The beginning of the tale made me smile so fine my heart turned as gold as the sunshine.
       When the sheep drank from the water crystal-like the thought came to me like a sword strike.
       When the sheep got lost in a dark place gloominess spread wildly across my face.
       When the Good Shepherd found the lost sheep happiness returned to me as though it couldn't sleep.
       And that's how the poem makes me feel inside with emotions so powerful they couldn't hide.

ST: That's a wonderful poem, J.

So, today, I wonder if you could tell me how you feel about the story today?

As you look back.

J: Well, it's quite amazing that the Good Shepherd keeps looking out for his sheep.

ST: Uh-huh.

How does that make you feel about the Good Shepherd?

J: It makes me happy cos I know that he'll never, ever go out with one sheep missing.

ST: Who do you think the Good Shepherd is?

J: Jesus.

ST: Jesus, right.

I think this is a really, really super piece of work. Why did you choose to write rather than do a picture?

J: Well, because I like poems, they're my sort of thing.

ST: Uh-huh.

That's good; you think you write better than you draw.

That was really good. Thank you.[7]

The two children above only had a single session for their entire Godly Play session, but the work that it produced was quite startling in its depth and understanding, as shown by the poem.

It may be that a child will spend several sessions working on a single piece; this will not be 'this week's' story but the child working on how the story touched her several sessions ago, work that needs time and energy to be completed and finished.

The children work on their own, until it is time to move into the next portion of time. The materials are designed so the children can be completely responsible for getting the materials out, then cleaning up and putting them away. Work in progress is stored. 'Finished' work can be taken away. All work is good, for the child has attended to her feelings and expressed them through the work.

Development: prayer

Once the work is put away, the children return to the circle for prayer. Again, this moves around the circle. Children may pray aloud or silently. Their 'Amen' is the cue to move on. A child who doesn't have a prayer may shake her head.

Development: the feast

The group then shares the feast: a drink and something to eat for each person. The children remain sitting in the circle while two of the group serve the feast, which is consumed together. The feast focuses on being together, not what is being consumed, in a clear reflection of the communion that the adults may be sharing at the same time in another place. So the children's community is built on the replaying of the overarching story of the Church, that of the Eucharist. The storyteller may talk with the children about other feasts that we know of from our scripture while the food is eaten, and then the children clear away, move back to the circle and wait for their parents or carers to collect them.

Ending and leaving

As with arriving, the departure is one at a time. The storyteller will say goodbye to every child, as will the greeter, and the children move off with their families.

Indirect learning

Throughout the session, the adults try to relate to each other consistently in a respectful, supportive and loving manner. The room is treated with respect and care; mess is cleaned up by whoever made it. 'We respect each other's work' is the clear rule. The adults also recognize that the children and the adults are there to learn from each other, and that listening, and giving time to the process of listening, is critical. This is the behaviour that we hope to inculcate in the children, and the indirect teaching that the children experience shows them how Christians of any age should be towards each other.

Enabling worship

The structure of the session reflects that of the Eucharist, which has come down to us through two thousand years of worship and tradition. Within the Eucharistic structure are the cues to help people into worship, and within the environment of the Godly Play space are similar visual and aural cues designed to help children to worship. The children are helped to come to the place where they can wonder, together and as individuals, and through that point of wonder the creativity of the child can interact with the Spirit of God, and learning can occur and be taken into the heart. The children form their own church, their own community, and draw from it as adults do from their own church. As with a Eucharist, the children come together. They greet each other; they share the story and wonder together, and develop their wondering about the story through play and creativity; they pray, share food and drink and then leave. Each moment of the time together is carefully maintained: personal, deliberate and thoughtful. The aim is that each child feels special, appreciated and known. The laid-back feel of each session is designed to help the children work just as much with their interior world as they do the external world. The measured pace of the session may feel quite weird for many who have worked in a more traditional style of Sunday school, or even one that is modelled on the education they see children experiencing during the week, but I have found this slow and thoughtful method to be very helpful, especially for children who tend to be rushing through life at the pace set all too often by busy parents or carers.

Godly Play aims to teach children how to use the language of the Christian tradition to encounter God and to use that encounter to gain direction for their lives. The sessions have been devised to enable children to come to God in a real and genuine manner, and to take their spiritual lives seriously. In previous work,[8] where I compared this method of storytelling with that of using puppets, it was evident that Godly Play did indeed enable the children to understand and internalize the story more effectively. I would heartily endorse this method for our week-by-week teaching in Sunday school whenever that is practicable.

Questions for discussion

1 How does the thought of this type of religious education strike you?
2 What aspects of Godly Play are new to you?
3 Are there any aspects of Godly Play that you find threatening?
4 Are there any aspects of the two conversations that surprised you? If so, can you share what they were with the rest of the group?
5 What practical constraints would your church or group encounter if you were to use Godly Play regularly?

8

Children thinking about God

———◆◆◆———

Throughout this book there are various comments from children about their spirituality and day-to-day experiences in the world. Most of them relate directly to God or to church, which ties down the breadth of spirituality that is present in children but gives an idea of how diverse children's thinking can be.

This chapter will look at some of the comments that I have collected recently,[1] trying to unpack what might lie behind each comment. I have arranged them in order of content and age, so we start with the youngest, hopefully seeing a more 'developed' image of God as the children's age increases. It may be beneficial to just remind yourself about Fowler's and Westerhoff's theories of faith development as well as the chapter on cognitive development, before reading on and seeing if you can relate what the children are saying, and their approach to God with what these two theories propose.

When I think about God I think about my little sister.

(George, 4)

George is a nursery–reception-aged child who has made a direct relationship between the God who creates and gives life and his little sister, about whom we know nothing. I'm assuming that George loves his sister, and that his feeling towards her and God is that of thankfulness and love. This comment (and most of the others) was logged just before Christmas, with the Christmas Nativity play happening daily in rehearsals, so it could be that George is thinking Christmas, baby, and so to sister.

It's a comment that shows an appreciation of the wonder of creation, love and family.

When I think about God I think about chickens.

(Oscar, 4)

This is simpler than it might seem at first! Oscar's family keep chickens, so I read here that Oscar thinks of home when he thinks about God. The word 'home' is a massive concept, which increases in complexity as you get older. For Oscar, though, home is a good place to be, with chickens. So thinking about God gives Oscar chickens on the mind. The other possible thread here is that chickens lay eggs and those are used for food, once again positive images of life and sustenance for a 4-year-old. There may even be a tie-in back to Easter and the images of eggs and new life.

I think about how lucky I am to have a loving family.

(Jordan, 11)

This gratitude for a loving home persists in Jordan at the top end of the school. God means loving family, with all the ramifications about security and bonding, and Jordan is now aware enough to know that not everyone has one of those – so he thanks God for this great base to work from. Jordan is equating God with love, love that is both given and received.

I think about God when my grandpa died and I was sad.

(Tamas, 6)

I think about God when I am all alone. I think about when I am dead.

(Tamara, 6)

I remember that he is making the world a very happy place. I remember when my mum told me about my great-grandfather fought in the war and how he is still alive now.

(Emily, 8)

I think about my grandad. His name was Sydney. I did not get to see him, he died.

(Sydney, 8)

We tend not to talk to children about death. We want to shield them from the pain and difficulty that adults inevitably have in dealing with death, so we pretend that children don't need to know about it. We also don't want to talk about death ourselves – this is a defining point about our present society – so we choose not to encourage children to go there either. In fact, children have interesting thoughts about death that can bring joy in the midst of grief, like the comment of a child seeing her deceased grandfather in the sun (page 70). They also have a lot of work to do in their own growing up that is concerned with recognizing death and their own mortality. They are aware that talking about death is hard for adults, and it's been my experience that once children know that I deal in death and bereavement, the questions come tumbling out. These are basic questions that children need to consider and ponder at their own speed. We need to be careful here about giving children the idea that adults don't talk about death any more than they talk about spirituality.[2] Our desire to protect our children from the tougher side of life is possibly doing more harm than we realize in the long term.

Christianity is predicated on the death of Jesus, and children entering churches will be met with crosses and depictions of the crucifixion. If our faith is based on the death and resurrection of God's Son, we must be prepared to help the children as they deal with the extraordinarily challenging idea of salvation and atonement. Christians are rarely honest about the complexity of this concept and area of belief; at theological college we studied ten different models of atonement, from the early Church until fairly recently, and I had problems relating to all of them! My favourite model is expounded in the (out-of-print) classic, *Can These Dry Bones Live?* by Frances Young.[3]

The conundrum of a Father God sending his Son to die is difficult enough for adults, let alone children. I firmly believe that we don't know, and probably couldn't get our heads around, what took place through that death and resurrection, other than that our relationship with God was changed for all time in a truly mysterious and incomprehensible way. My personal belief is that to teach the more simplistic, formulaic, version of salvation is possibly not going to help anyone, but to help children struggle and work towards a great mystery is probably a better thing to do. It's allowing the Spirit of God to work within the child's imagination, and that's a risky business, but I firmly believe that the Spirit of God is better working with a child's faith than my words. If you find that challenging, then so do I!

One of the things children find difficult, as do we all, is picturing what a soul is like. When my own 4-year-old wanted to know where his (deceased) granny was and what had happened to her body, I tried to explain along the lines that she didn't need her body any more, so only the bit that made her Granny was still alive, and that was with God in heaven. He replied, 'So she's like a ball, bouncing around?'

A helpful image that a friend gave me when I repeated the above story is to talk of the dead person leaving their body behind rather like taking off a layer of clothes.[4]

Children appreciate that living things die, and that something of a person (or, as far as a child is concerned, pet) continues with God. Hence the relating of God and death that we see from Tamas. Children realize quite young that their parents will die too, leaving them in the world. This is a huge issue for children to come to terms with, and best handled with care, but always let them talk when they need to about this difficult area.

In my collection of children's thinking, death frequently occurs. Children need to be taken seriously when they ask about death, not fobbed off. Tamara is quite clearly aware of her mortality and is musing on it, but her thinking about death is difficult for me to contemplate – I might try to change her subject to 'something a little more cheerful'. But why should I assume that Tamara is being morbid? The problem is within us and our culture that likes to avoid thinking about our own mortality. That such a discussion reminds the adult of his or her own mortality (which may have very different connotations from a child's mortality) is undoubtedly why we try to turn the conversation.

Emily is older, and finds the idea of eternal life a great comfort when trying to deal with the problem of her forbears being dead, yet part of her parents' memories. She may also have realized the comfort that this gives to her mother. Sydney is clearly pleased to share his grandad's name, despite never having met the older Sydney. Again, thinking about God helps when thinking about death and our mortality, as the clear belief here is that Sydney Jr will eventually meet Sydney Sr.

This ability to be with difficult thoughts which pertain to the spiritual is indicative of the children's own vast resources in the area of spirituality, and their intuitive understanding is in startling contrast to that of most adults.

I think about God when I am alone in the dark and I am scared without anyone with me.

(Abigail, 6)

Abigail is scared of the dark. So am I, if I'm honest, and our hearts go out to her as she speaks of her fear. It's a natural instinct to be scared of the dark; you were more likely to be eaten in the night than in the day, as our eyes don't work so well then and the night is the resting time for humans. The other aspect to being scared now is our natural creativity. If I wasn't busy imagining what might be under the bed or creeping up the stairs, I wouldn't be so frightened.

But Abigail thinks about God at this time, the one person who is there in the dark with her when she's alone. God is acting here as a parent or friend: someone to be there for her at a time when she would otherwise be lonely. Night time is traditionally associated with God dealing with people; it was in the time when they were alone that God spoke to many of the prophets in the Bible, and later to Mary and to Zechariah. People interviewed in more recent days acknowledge more spiritual experiences when they are alone. Being alone in the dark opens our minds, as we can't see images to control our thoughts. Our creativity is given expression through our imaginative thoughts, and then again our deepest selves can speak to us through our dreams. It's a good and natural thing to think about God when we're alone in the dark.

When I think of God, it makes me happy and I say prayers to him and he listens to me all the time! Thank you, God!

(Joshua, 7)

Joshua's comment is charmingly worded, but is concerned with Joshua and what God does for him and contrasts with Kamran's comment below. But Joshua is typical of a child of this age, and it's worth looking at what he has to say. Piaget points out to us that children of this age are egocentric. Parents can never give them all the time that the child would take if given open access, but God can be there, 100 per cent for Joshua. God listens to Joshua all the time! Joshua has understood that God is there for him always, and his faith is shining through. Joshua says his prayers, which are, I assume, very much of the 'God bless Mummy and Daddy' type, but are important for him. Certainly the prayers at assembly with children of this age are of necessity quite simple, although they don't need to be simplistic.[5] Children of this age will write prayers that tend to be one-liners, usually quite profound and to the point. Joshua's comment is also worth noting because God makes him happy – this is a very up-beat contribution. How many adult Christians act as if – or say that – God makes them happy?

I think that he is strong and lovely and cares for all of us.

(Kamran, 7)

In Kamran's comment we see several aspects of a child's understanding of God's personality. First, God is male, both in the 'he' and the 'strong' (which could be used about a woman, but probably wouldn't be) and then we also have 'God is lovely' – a lovely person or lovely to look at? Does it matter? It's an unusual adjective to use about God, and usually ascribed to a woman. And finally, God cares for us. Put the whole thing together, and the gender of God is far more blurred: lovely, strong and caring. Kamran's comment is imaginative and very affectionate in its tone. In terms of his concept of God, Kamran is progressing well towards his own internalized understanding; this is not as egocentric as many comments from children of this age. If we contrast this with Joshua's comment, you see the breadth of spiritual understanding in children of this age. This may be affected by the households that the two boys come from (but which I do not know; the following comment arises from hunch, not knowledge); a strongly religious family would, through ongoing conversations and practice, enable children to work on their concept of God in a way that would not be so accessible to a child from a more secular background.

A helpful, caring man.

(Charlie, 8)

I think of an old man in the clouds.

(Joseph, 8)

I think of God sitting high on his throne watching down on us.

(Isobel, 9)

Charlie, Isobel and Joseph articulate the classic child's view of God. Where does this view come from? We don't have the beard, but we have the old man on the throne.

Many children go through this stage, reflecting a distance between us and God, and will also say that heaven is 'up there'. Perhaps this comes from images of God seen in pictures – the Sistine Chapel, Blake's *God Creating Adam* – or perhaps the most powerful people that they know are kings and queens, who tend to be imagined as older, on thrones. Helpful and caring give us the classic 'grandfather' concept of God. Notice that these children don't seem to have heard about the God who sits in judgment, although a distant God could be read in these comments, a God who is watching rather than acting.

I wonder what he does and what he looks like.

(Ciaran, 8)

Ciaran's comment appeals to me enormously – a child wondering in an open and honest way about what God is really like and what he does. Ciaran has appreciated that God is not like us and doesn't 'work' as we do, so what does he do? How does God do his work? And what is he really like? This is an open and very attractive spirituality. The problem for me is that I would like to suggest the answers to Ciaran – and why should I presume to know the answers? These are questions that the wise will leave to the young to answer. The way to help Ciaran move on might be to ask carefully worded questions of the 'I wonder' variety, to help Ciaran think through his thoughts about the activity of God in the world, and whether God 'looks like' anything that we might recognize at all.

I see Jesus and him in my mind in heaven together.

(Henry, 8)

Henry has moved on to purely Christian thinking about God. Jesus is seemingly a more straightforward concept than God, so to think about Jesus with God marks Henry's thinking as more specifically Christian than the thoughts we have encountered so far. The fact of Jesus is very important within the Christian faith, as Jesus gives God an (imagined) face, and the historical reality of a person, like people we see in our day-to-day lives. For members of other faiths, this insight into the person of God must be quite enviable. For those who are forbidden to make any sort of representation of God, Jesus must seem like a real bonus! The big negative of Jesus is that he underlines the male gender of God that we keep seeing in these children's comments and that most of them will hold on to as they grow older.

> *I love God, and that he will be looking after my brother in heaven.*

(Ellie, 8)

This comment brings us back to the story of St Freddie. It is still a horrible fact of life that some people die young and some babies don't get to grow up. Ellie's brother and Freddie are two such early deaths that left sisters trying to come to terms with the baby brother who died. Having a belief in God who looks after the dead is surely of great value to these children. When they get older they may then ask the unanswerable 'why', but as yet they haven't got to that stage. People who can ask 'why' and get no answer yet still hold on to their faith have entered Fowler's Stage 4 and may well have travelled through it to Stage 5, being usually many years older than Ellie.

A friend who had a miscarriage suffered from recurring depression for years after the event. Eventually, she asked God to show her the lost child, and she had a dream in which the baby was now the right age – he was about 7. So she accepted that, eventually, she would meet the child who died so young, and that his life hadn't actually ended with his earthly death: he was growing up in heaven.

For many Christians, this belief that we meet our loved ones again after our own death is very important. When dealing with our own bereavements, such a belief can be a real anchor in the storm of grief. Children seem to have no problem with the concept of continuity, including the idea that life could 'begin' before we are born, in our heavenly existence that prefigures earthly life.

There is nothing wrong or bad about God.

(Callum B, 8)

This is the classic comment from a child, in that no adult would say this. Read it again, and appreciate the purity of the child-like faith. Callum clearly has an understanding of what is wrong or bad, and he defines God by saying God is not that.[6] He could have said that God is good and right, and an adult might choose to use longer words to say the same thing, but Callum defines God by excluding the qualities that he recognizes as sinful (although I wonder if he even knows that word?). There is a real sense of awe in this simple statement, and of understanding the truth about what is in the heart of God. It is to such as these that the kingdom of heaven belongs.

When I think about God I be [sic] silent.

(Callum C, 8)

This comment comes from another Callum and once again resonates with insight. As above, this Callum is developing a sense of God that is awesome, that is beginning to delve into the abstract, the infinite nature of God. It is usually a mature adult Christian who says that when they think of God, they come to silence. This child modestly writes his few words that might sum up years of pilgrimage.

'When I think of God . . .'

I picture angels gliding around a light in a dark and starry place.

(Emelye, 8)

I see a king on a throne but he doesn't have a crown or a cloak, he is just dressed the same as the other people.

(Ryan, 9)

I imagine what he looks like and think if he is a lady or a man or even a thing, (but not an animal).

(Gregor, 9)

I think that he is not in the sky, he is in the world.

(Mitchell, 9)

I think of massive light and clouds and everyone lives life to the extreme.

(Sam, 9)

Can you hear the thinking processes going on in this selection? These are children who are all about the same age, and we clearly see that some of them have lost the image of God in the sky, while others are still there. The angels in the dark and starry place is the simple view of heaven as up in the sky. The king on the throne, but dressed as other people, shows that the idea of God's kingship being different is fomenting in Ryan's mind. If God isn't a king like a regular king, then what is God like? Children of this age often describe people by their exterior, so we have the comment about cloaks and crowns. Gregor is still puzzled by the bodily appearance of God – everyone else he knows is either male or female, and while God can be a thing, God can't be an animal. It's worth staying with Gregor: this is a really honest comment, clearly showing his concepts being ratcheted into the next stage of Piagetian cognitive theory. Gregor understands that God cannot be categorized in the way that everything else that he has come across can. And this is the only comment that I received from this cohort of children to the effect that God could be either male or female, but God's probably neither.

Ryan and Gregor are both in the process of moving from the king on the throne towards what we see in Mitchell's comment – he's not in the sky, he is in the world. Mitchell's God is omnipresent, and again unique to this cohort of children.

Sam's comments about life to the extreme (perhaps a paraphrase of John 10.10, 'I came that they may have life, and have it abundantly', or perhaps too much 'extreme sport' on the computer at home!) are unusual. Sam sees life with God as more; more extreme is hard to comprehend without talking further with Sam, but he clearly sees that the life of faith has advantages over that of no faith. Light is always a positive image, and Sam sees the light as God. Interestingly, there are also clouds, perhaps to hide behind, or perhaps to make the picture of the sunny summer sky. Perhaps the clouds reflect Sam's learning that life has good and bad patches, but that God is with Sam no matter what.[7]

> *I think that if God didn't exist then we would not exist either so I think of that every time someone mentions God.*
>
> (Andrew, 9)

> *I say to myself, 'I wouldn't be here, if God didn't make the world.'*
>
> (Oliver, 9)

> *I ask myself all sorts of questions about God. What is he like? Will I ever see him? Will I go to heaven or hell?*
>
> (Shaquille, 10)

> *I think he is like the key to the world and without him the world wouldn't be a good place to live.*
>
> (Caroline, 9)

This group of children fix their ideas of God in that of the almighty creator, the omnipotent God. There are the beginnings of real philosophical thought taking root, as these children chew the cud internally over the question of the nature of God. They are clearly well into the third stage of Piagetian thought, with concrete operations evident in the way that they are thinking and expressing themselves. The children are still clearly committed to God being there, and not seeming to doubt God's existence yet, although the questions are the precursors of some of the big philosophical and religious questions that we all confront: does God exist? What is the nature of God really like? How can we find out? Some of the children have begun to enter this later, more questioning stage:

I think of God always looking over the world and he's the happiness inside us.

(Kirsty, 11)

He sits in a golden circle which is heaven looking at the whole earth.

(Alexander, 10)

I think that God and I are in a garden, chatting to each other about flowers in the garden.

(Megan, 10$\frac{1}{2}$)

I think about God as a huge hand coming with blinding light and gives me comfort when I die where I'll go.

(Chris, 10)

I think of a face in the clouds, watching everyone and everything.

(Emma, 11)

I think of a bright spiritual light shining among entire darkness.

(Alex, 11)

I find him like the Godfather of the world. A great big powerful man.

(Tom, 11)

In this selection of comments from children in the same age group at school, the big differences are clearly showing between them. The comments vary from a quite sophisticated idea, of the golden circle around the globe, to the Godfather image, which I find rather scary! From the face in the clouds through the Godfather to the huge hand with blinding light, these children are tussling with God internally, working on a definition for the indefinable. The awe that we have seen so much previously is still evident, and the nature of God is shifting even more towards the omnipotent. I wonder if these children would still give me such open views in a year's time, when they've begun at a secondary school, their hormones have started to rage and peer pressure to conform to the secular norm is becoming stronger.

I become calm!

(Brandon, 11)

My hopes and pleads seem to come true and my worries go away.

(James, 11)

I see myself with him.

(Jack, 9)

These short, simple statements are very pleasing to read. These reflect for me a healthy faith in these children. Calm feelings, prayers coming true and worries receding, seeing oneself with God – these children are talking of a real relationship with God in an honest and affecting manner. These are children who have learned about faith and have now internalized and own their faith.

I think about whether he is real or not, and if he is, what does he look like?

(Eleanor, 9)

Eleanor is displaying the classic existential thought: does God exist? Some would say that the fact that Eleanor is wondering whether God exists tells us that, actually, God must do, as we clearly spend a lot of time wondering about this thing we call God.[8] Yet she still wonders what God looks like. Is this a feature of the society that we live in, where appearances are so important, and, as previously mentioned, especially important to children? In a few years, when she has, for the moment, come to an answer as to whether God exists, we need to ask Eleanor again whether it matters what God looks like. For now, she is still thinking about a God who has some sort of bodily attributes. Eleanor's wondering is healthy and good; the fact of her wondering shows us that her spiritual life is alive and well.

I don't believe in God.

(Louie, 10)

I don't believe in God, because he would have stopped all war.

(Mikiel, 10)

I don't really believe in him because I think, how was God made, how did God come to be?

(Ellis, 10)

Well, I don't think about God. In assembly I don't say the prayer.

(Arun, 10)

If God is almighty, why doesn't he answer our prayers or help?
(Alex, 10)

So we arrive at a group of children who have decided to give up childish ways. Of the entire cohort, only one other response like this was present, from a 4-year-old, who replied, '*I don't know*.' Maybe it's cheating, but I read that as 'I don't know about God' rather than 'I don't believe in God,' while this group have decided, for reasons that we hear all around us, that God doesn't exist at all. Ellis's wondering about who made God is a classic in a child often younger than Ellis, and not something that adults often say.

I'm pleased these children felt able to be truthful in this way, and that they have now arrived at a faith that excludes God. Bearing in mind that the school they attend is strongly Christian, it's great that these children have come to a real questioning of God, and felt able to reflect that to me. (Remember, you don't have to believe in God to have faith, or to have a personal spirituality that is alive and well.) Giving children permission to say what they really think, rather than what they think

I want them to say, is critical, but hard to achieve in the present school system. How do I know the other children were being honest and not just writing down what they thought they wanted me to hear them say? This wanting to please, and give 'the right answer', as well as going along with the rest of the group, was bound to skew some of the comments that the children have made.

My concern is always whether these really are the children's thought-through decisions, or if they are merely copying the words that they hear around them at school and at home.

However, there were a few comments that I would like to finish with that need a little more unpacking, as they refer back to work that I had previously entered into with the children, usually quite a long time before.

I think of sheep and purple velvet robes.

(Victoria, 11)

Every year, I work with the Year 6 children in RE when they are studying the 'I am' statements of Jesus. I go in and tell them the story of the Good Shepherd (John 10 mixed with Psalm 23), using Godly Play as the method.[9] This was many months ago, and it has clearly fixed in Victoria's mind. She does not say in what context she thinks of sheep, and who the sheep stand for, but this is a comment about the value of Godly Play as a teaching method. Victoria clearly internalized the parable when she heard it told a good while before.

The purple velvet robes? This must be a reflection on Easter and the story of Good Friday, which was eight months previous to the time of her comment. The purple robes paired with the sheep represent an unusual combination.

Both of these comments illustrate the way children hold things in their minds, often for far longer than an adult would. When I was in school researching for some writing, I used the 'Good Shepherd' Godly Play as previously. One child drew a picture of the disciples, including Judas hanging himself. This seemed at first to have little relationship to the Good Shepherd or the season, which was just before Christmas. For eight months this lad had been thinking, albeit probably at a subconscious level, about Judas hanging himself. My work that day gave him the opportunity to open up and work on that disturbing story once more. As adults, we find this challenging, but as adults who work regularly with children we should always be open and alert to children referring to stories and events that we have dusted down and stored away many weeks previously.

> *Jesus is the saviour of the world. A candle burns with holy fire; when the candle is blown out, the fire is gone. Jesus is gone, but he will return again.*
>
> (Charlotte, 9)

On Ascension Day, I took a candle into school, and based my assembly story around the Godly Play story of the Ascension – a difficult concept for adults, let alone children.[10] Charlotte's comments tell the story pretty much as I did. A lit candle stands for Jesus, the light of the world. The candle was extinguished using an egg cup 'snuffer' and we watched the smoke curl upward and outwards, and then smelt the air. The explanation is that the flame hasn't gone, it's just changed as it goes out. Charlotte has fed the story back to me, seven months after she heard it. I think that's pretty remarkable!

Be encouraged when stories don't seem to be instantly 'successful'; this assembly was regarded by the staff as one of my more unusual ones, and they seemed fairly perplexed at the end. Yet Charlotte has held on to it, and that way of telling the story has fed Charlotte, once again, for many months.

I hope these comments are useful to you; taking time to unpack the seemingly simple comments of children is a worthwhile exercise, and helps us to see God through their eyes. It draws us nearer to understanding children understanding God.

Questions for discussion

1 Share some of the comments that your children have made with each other, and see if you can take the children's comments and reflect on them together. What is God saying to you through these children?

2 How do you handle children who want to talk about death?

3 What seems to be the predominant 'hang-up' with the children that you work with? How do you stay with the children in their concern, helping them to work on the issue?

4 What can you remember of your Sunday school teaching? What does this tell you about the best way to approach your own children?

9

The way forward

When I was little, I was always aware of other things: other atmospheres, entities, feelings. Like, I was aware that I wasn't alone in a room, even when there was no other human being there. When you're a child – especially when you're a toddler – you're much more susceptible to that kind of thing, because you just accept it's there.
(Tracey Emin, interviewed in the *Church Times*,
1 December 2006)

When I trained to be a teacher, I spent three years learning my profession, and before that I was interviewed before I was accepted to train. Then,

- I worked on subject specific studies, so I knew more science than the children I was teaching.
- I worked on professional studies, so I knew how to actually stand up in a classroom and teach.
- I worked on educational studies, so I knew about child development.
- I was judged through essays and reviews, teaching practice and examination.
- I had a first year of teaching, where I had a mentor and was helped to deal with the difficulties and stresses of the post.[1]

People entering teaching now are all graduates, with a good level of English and maths. Sunday school teachers are volunteers, often young people who like working with children. There is no question of interviewing Sunday school teachers, as ministers and churches are just too pleased to have them volunteer! We submit a Criminal Records Bureau (CRB) search to ensure these volunteers have no criminal record, and then they work with the children.

How many churches have study groups for these people, to ensure that they are also growing as Christians? After all, these people don't even hear sermons, as they are out with the kids. Quite a few Sunday school teachers are actually the parents of the children they are teaching, and may have little more knowledge of the Christian faith than their children. While this is often a great way to learn the faith, are they actually learning and growing in the best environment for them? How do they articulate the questions that might arise for them?

How many Sunday school teachers have on-the-job training, a mentor or even some help from time to time? How many get time with their minister to check that things are going well within the children's work in this church?

I realize that I'm painting a 'worst-case scenario' here, but I want to raise the subject of how ill equipped and supported most of our children's workers are, through no fault of their own. It is the churches, and their leaders, who have let these wonderful, generous people down. If we are to equip Sunday school teachers and children's workers properly to work within churches, then each church needs to take a pace backwards and engage with the most fundamental questions:

- Why do we separate the children out from the rest of the worshipping community?
- What do we want for the children?
- Who should be working with the children?
- How do we equip these people to work with the children?
- How does the church support our children's workers?
- How do we ensure that the needs of these people are being met, to prevent 'burnout' or people being institutionalized to the extent that they won't leave the teaching role to join the regular congregation 'in the pews'?

Why do we separate out the children?

This is taken for granted at most churches; the adults have the main building, and the children are taken out, sometimes across a busy road, to their own version of church elsewhere. There is good sense in taking out the children, so let's look at that first:

- Children think differently from adults (see Chapter 2). So it's good for them to learn the Christian faith with work that is designed for them. Adults would find working at this level fine for a week or two, and then they'd want to get on with more intellectual aspects, such as reflecting on the more difficult areas of faith.
- Children have different patterns of behaviour. They find sitting still for more than a few moments hard, and have not been socialized to tolerate such discomfort, as adults have. If they are in church for a service that has been designed with adults in mind, they may well 'misbehave'. We don't expect children of 7 to read Dickens, so we shouldn't expect them to be able to access adult worship in the way that adults do.[2] Children can take from the adult liturgy, but only in short bursts. One of my choristers often talks to me about my sermons – and he's been doing this since he was about 9. Most of the junior choristers describe the service as 'boring', and I'm not surprised.

So, if we want the children to stay for the whole service, then the service needs to be 'slanted' towards their needs. Adults can access and understand liturgy designed for children, but that's not reversible; children do not usually have the cognitive processes required for adult liturgies. This needs to be borne in mind when 'all-age' liturgies are being planned, and if it really is to be 'all-age' then something different for several age groups will be needed at the teaching slot if all those present are to be stretched and their worshipping needs met.

What are the constraints of your building?

Have you ever considered swapping who gets the church on a Sunday? Taking the adults out to wherever the children's work usually goes on, and seeing what they say as they creep back at the appropriate part of the service? I can hear the 'harrumphing' now!

Children are taken out because of two criteria. One is purely pragmatic, to do with getting folk in. The other is to do with thinking processes.

Most churches were designed to seat as many as possible. Hopefully your church was originally designed to be flexible, or has had some remedial reordering to make it more accommodating. If you have pews, it's even more difficult to create a truly child-friendly church; we recommend parents with lively children to sit in the pews with pillars, which cut off the escape route for the child! I can remember hiding under the pew one particularly boring day in church as a small child. And I was so well behaved as a child – the service must have been dreadful that day. Pews do have advantages: you can always cram in another person at Christmas, and they're easier to keep clean. Replacing pews with chairs in rows, aping pews, is, in my opinion, a fine waste of money.[3]

An area somewhere in the church where harassed parents can take their small child to potter and play is great, but do site it where the parent can still access the worship and feel part of the community; if they'd wanted to play with their child they'd be better off at the local park. The best thing for parents of small children is a crèche, sited away from the worship, so parents can really engage with some spiritual food. They probably need it more than any other generation. But we're talking about yet another space here, and your church may be at capacity with the older children out in Sunday school.

How many rooms or spaces do you have for Sunday school? This will probably dictate how many groups you have – and how many teachers. We need to think, therefore, about the children's needs, and see how we can come to the best compromise of what we want and what we can host, given the physical constraints.

What do we want for the children?

This question is at the heart of all children's work, but I guess is not often asked; we tend to assume we all know what we're about. The word 'assume' is interesting: take it apart and you can see what an *ass* you make *me* . . . always check out assumptions about children's work.

Sit down with your team and brainstorm what they think we want for our children. There are lots of issues here, and I hope they will all surface. Some will be:

- Christian education;
- faith formation;
- a secure place to explore their spirituality;
- a safe place to encounter the church;
- worship that is fun;
- age-related teaching;
- friendships;
- stories;
- a place to pray;
- fellowship for the adults as well as the children;
- somewhere that the children can just 'be';
- mission towards the families from which the children come.

Note these down on an OHP or flip-chart as they come up.

The next question will be along the lines of:

How do we provide these?

Group your answers to the above into related answers. Some are to do with the children's Christian education, some to do with personal development. Some are to do with their relationship to the Church, others to do with creating a safe place for children to develop as spiritual people. Categorize them as it seems best to you; this is not an enforced list! You will then need to chat about which items of your list are the key criteria. All are important, or they wouldn't be there, but you need to pare down your list, or at least prioritize it so that you can start at the most important and work downwards.

Once you've got your basic list of priorities, you need to brainstorm once more. Here comes the other side of the coin. This time, ask your team:

What are the constraints?

These will be comments such as:

- There's a lack of people to work with the children.
- Physical constraints – we've only one room.
- Our Sunday school scheme is boring.
- We need someone to help us with the singing.
- The children misbehave.
- No one wants to help because then they miss out on church.
- We run on a shoestring budget (what budget?).
- Children do too much on Sundays – we don't have enough children.
- Parents just want to 'dump' their children and don't encourage them or take any interest.
- Children are only here on alternate weekends because they are off to Mum's or Dad's every other weekend.

Be creative

Now you get the creative part; somehow these two lists have to be brought together to give the way forward. It might be useful to duplicate the lists and give a copy to everyone. Agree to pray over the lists for a few days, and then reconvene the meeting. Time, and especially sleep, often help the brain to square a circle. Creativity rises during our sleeping, and one of your team, or a combination, may well provide some original thinking as to how the group should go forward.

During your second meeting, the decisions need to be made as to how you fit your hopes and needs with the reality of what you've got. Bear in mind the following points from this book:

- Children at different cognitive stages benefit from being in different groups for teaching and socializing, so try to have a group for rising 5s, one for 5–7s and one for 7–11s (7–9 and 9–11 ideally).
- Try to give different groups a contained space, so they don't hear each other or spill into each other's area.
- Try to give each group a gender balance in its teachers.
- Encourage all your teachers to undertake some sort of basic training (through diocesan or area structures).
- Vary the adults who tell stories to your children; many adults who wouldn't agree to be part of the teaching team can tell stories – ask them in to 'do a turn'.
- Use the institutional structures, such as Diocesan Children's Officers, to help your group. Get them to lead workshops, speak at all-age events, lead training days. That's what they're for.
- Don't forget Child Protection measures. There will be guidelines and rules for this. Ask your minister if he or she is not breathing down your neck about it.

Draw up a 'wish list'

Make the compromises that need to be made, but also draw up a 'wish list' for the future; a bit like my 'aims and objectives' (see Chapter 10). Your hopes and dreams may contain some of the following:

- Next year increase numbers of 5- to 7-year-olds by 20 per cent.
- Try a new work scheme when this one expires (usually at Advent).

- Send two teachers on a Godly Play course.
- Have a children's party in the summer.
- Start a mid-week group at the local school in two years' time.

Your compromises may look like:

1 Mission statement: this Sunday club is for children first and foremost. We aim to provide a safe environment in which the children can
   (a) worship God, through Jesus Christ, in the power of the Holy Spirit;
   (b) grow up as Christians;
   (c) explore their own spirituality through story, prayer and creative activity;
   (d) experience a caring and compassionate ethos;
   (e) be valued for who they are;
   (f) have fun!
2 The group aims to act as a supportive resource for the children's families. We do this through meeting weekly
   (a) to worship God together and with the wider congregation in church;
   (b) to hear stories and work on their meaning in age-related groups;
   (c) to play games;
   (d) to sing, dance and act;
   (e) to be creative together;
   (f) to share our learning with the wider congregation, and to help leading the all-age services;
   (g) to listen to the children, and hear what God is saying to us through them.

For me, that last one is the critical objective. It says publicly that this is not a baby-sitting service, it is a place where we take children and their needs seriously, and we value what they bring to us.

Who should be working with the children?

For many churches, this is a matter of whoever volunteers. Expectation is often that the children's parents help with them. This is not always a good idea:

- The parents may well want a break from their children.
- The children will behave differently if their parents are present.
- This can also cause role confusion for the parent. Are they seeming to 'favour' their own child against another? What if there's a fight including their child? What happens if their child wants a cuddle halfway through the story?

It's not ideal. Only go down this route if the parent understands what the drawbacks could be.

Basics

- All people working with children must have CRB clearance.
- There is no upper age limit, but no one under 18 can be left alone with children.
- There should always be two people with each group of children, or within sight and sound of each other, to handle emergencies, and to provide back-up for each other. You are far less likely to be accused of acting in an unprofessional manner if there's a witness. And it's scriptural: Jesus sent his disciples out two by two. You need a companion on your journey with these children.
- Ideally there should also be a spare pair of hands to help out when needed, even if it's just taking Eloise to the toilet.

Many people expect people who work as teachers to do this work at church. Just think about that – is it fair? It may well cause role confusion for a child who is taught by Mr Hussein during the week to then find him at Sunday school too, but called Ali.

And Mr Ali Hussein probably wants a break from his day job on a Sunday. If a teacher doesn't offer, my advice is don't ask them!

It's very good for everyone if you can get a gender balance. Traditionally Sunday school teaching is seen as 'women's work' but that may be presenting working with the children, especially if it's in the hall down the road, as less important than what goes on with the adults. If we really think working with the children is important, we need to see the clergy helping too, be they male or female, and a good age range and mix of people teaching and supporting our children. Many of them desperately need a male role model, and this is a great opportunity. Do be aware of the children getting the unspoken message that church is for women, and older women at that. They do make up the largest contingent in the congregation, and if the children are taught by older women only, that is the message you are giving them.

Be aware of the personalities of your teaching team. If everyone is an activist, who is going to help the more reflective children? If all the teachers are extrovert, how will the introverted, shy children cope? You need to ensure a mix of people, with different skills and abilities. Don't let the group self-select people who they get on with all the time, or you'll find a certain sort of personality beginning to dominate; while the team will get on, some children could feel excluded as they will not find that special person who is 'like me'. It's good for the team to have to work at managing the personalities contained within it – that's life, and that's the Church too. And never think an elderly, quiet woman would not be an asset. Surrogate grannies and grandads are a boon to today's children.

How do we equip these people to work with the children?

Everyone needs some basic training.

- Do they agree with the mission statement and the aims and objectives for the group?
- Do they know the basics of child development? If not, give them this book to read!
- Do they know what they will be doing as part of the team? Do they have a job description?
- Are they familiar with the policy for managing difficult or unacceptable behaviour? Basic training can be given by asking the volunteer to help with the group before he takes on a group of his own. An experienced teacher can act as a 'mentor' for the volunteer until he feels confident. Few volunteers haven't had small children of their own at some point, so an awful lot will be intuitive, but it's good to give the opportunity for feedback and discussion.
- Do you have a fellowship group that meets specifically for the Sunday school team? If not, perhaps it's time you did! A monthly meeting, partly to discuss the curriculum for the next few weeks, and then to attend to the adults' spirituality, is a good team-builder as well as ensuring that the teachers are growing as Christians too![4]
- It's important that the person in charge gets to see the various 'off-the-shelf' materials that are produced for Sunday schools. Good Christian bookshops will stock these, and may let you take them on a 'sale or return' basis to share with the others. A change often is beneficial, as the children will experience different styles and resources.
- Make sure the church pays for any materials that the group needs. A budget is essential and really underlines the church's commitment to the work with children. 'Subs' are

a good idea; use these to pay for luxuries, such as drinks and biscuits, and that new piece of carpet that you've been talking about buying for five years . . .

- Encourage all your teachers to sign up for ongoing training, be it once a week, once a fortnight or just annually.
- Encourage all of your teachers to attend at least one full day of Godly Play training. They will find it enormously enriching personally as well as in terms of working with the children.

How does the church support our children's workers?

Do your congregation have any idea of what goes on in the children's groups? Communication is the key.

- Include articles by the children in the church magazine.
- Put your children's work up around the church.
- Conduct interviews with the children as well as their teachers as part of the worship.
- If you have a series of photos of people with roles in the church, are your Sunday school teachers included?
- Make sure the children's work has a budget set by your PCC or church committee, and that there is a children's work report for your AGM.
- Do you regularly pray for your children's workers, and for the children?
- Do you 'commission' your children's workers at the beginning of each year, be it at Advent or when the schools return after the summer break, or even at the beginning of January?
- Ensure the group has its own notice area in church, and refer the rest of the congregation to it.

- Invite the Sunday school to take part when the church is being decorated for special events and festivals. Who said there's an age limitation on flower arranging?
- Don't forget the group for the teachers, to ensure their spirituality doesn't dry up due to a lack of adult teaching and fellowship.

How do we ensure that the needs of these people are being met?

This is needed to prevent 'burnout', or people being institutionalized to the extent that they won't leave the teaching role to join the regular congregation 'in the pews'.

There's an old joke: old fishermen never die, they only smell that way. What happens to older Sunday school teachers? How do we prevent this peculiar type of institutionalization, where folk who have given years to work with children find that they cannot stop? Many people who have always been in some sort of role in church discover that losing that role means they find it hard to worship with everyone else. It is particularly noticeable in choristers, who often look very uncomfortable in the regular pews, as do retired organists and clergy. But for now, let's just think about Sunday school teachers.

What do you do if your Sunday school superintendent or person in charge doesn't want to retire, and it looks to you, and many others, that she seems to be past her 'sell by' date in this ministry?

This will be excruciatingly hard, no matter how good you are at your pastoral work. Let's look at it from the person's standpoint:

I don't understand it. I've given years of my life to teaching the children. I love doing it and the children love me too, or at least, I thought they did. Of course I find it hard, getting to church before everyone else, setting it all out, doing the preparation: the reading, the thinking and praying, duplicating worksheets, raiding my store cupboard for craft materials. But I love it, and I'm sure God called me to do this 15 years ago (or maybe 30, 45 . . . years ago) and I haven't heard him say it's time to give it all up. Yes, the children do seem more lively now, but they seem to like doing the puzzles and reading the books that I give them. I just don't see why I can't continue.

Even people who want to give up find it hard to let go. This is where they've been for many years, and the children are very dear to them. They may not know the new people in church. They may find the service wordy and different from how it used to be. They may fret that the new person doesn't understand what Jack means when he looks like that . . .

All change is difficult. Letting go of a role that defined a person, and possibly gave them power in a small group, is very hard to do.

Perhaps the best way to prevent this is to ask people to teach for a set number of years, with a regular review, so that there is a turnover of people, a bit like serving as a school governor (or on the PCC if you're Anglican). This may ruffle feathers when instigated but will be appreciated by the volunteers, who can see that they're not signing up to be with the children for the rest of their lives. Younger volunteers may well recognize this business pattern and be fine with the idea.

As well as this, you may be able to form a team of workers who are each only with the children perhaps once a month, each with their own week, and you can see how that goes. If they say, 'Well, I'd rather be in with the children every week,' stick to your guns and explain that doing that isn't fair on Maisie, who's in charge that week. And even if the person replies that Maisie's said that she's fine with him being there, put your foot down, and say that you really want Maisie to have a crack at it without him – how else will Maisie get the confidence that she needs? In other words, be wise as a serpent, and gentle as a dove. Be aware that if the person really doesn't want to stop, and you feel that he really needs to, you may indeed have to break the egg to make the omelette. Always be aware that you must hold the interests of the children paramount.

If this chapter has challenged you profoundly and you feel like running away rather than engaging with the whole agenda, then only start this year! Tackle the changes slowly and prayerfully, with your minister on board. Remember, it's the children that we're here for, and they'll be the beneficiaries.

Questions for you to consider

1 What changes would you like to see within your Sunday school?
2 What difficulties do you foresee if you try to set these changes in motion?
3 What support would you like in your work? How could you ensure it's there for you?

10

A sharing of 'good practice'

————◆◆◆————

I'm not part of the body, cos I don't get any bread.
(James, aged 4, at communion, in response to the bidding,
'We break this bread to share in the body of Christ.
Though we are many, we are all one body
because we all share one bread.')

This chapter is offered as a pattern of how to proceed with a possibly difficult issue, outlining how to manage both adults and children in the process, but more importantly giving an example of a 'mixed media' course for children.

In the spring of 2006, my church took the decision to admit children to communion prior to their being confirmed. This chapter outlines the process by which the church arrived at that decision, and then the course that I devised with my curate to lead the children up to the great day itself. Should your church decide to go down this path, please contact your Diocesan Children's Officer, or equivalent, for guidance as to how you should proceed.

Issues around children receiving communion prior to confirmation include:

- At baptism, children become full members of the Christian Church. Surely that should include receiving communion, as in the Orthodox Church?
- Children perceive not receiving communion as excluding them, not taking them seriously. Offering this to them gives concrete action to our words of acceptance.

- If children receive communion, confirmation then becomes an adult rite of joining the Church and of owning their faith, not the 'gate to communion' that it is at present.
- When adults comment that 'Children don't understand', I query how many of us understand this means of grace? And why should an adult's understanding be more desirable than that of a child? What about adults with learning difficulties?
- The experience of churches that have allowed children to receive has been very positive, both in terms of the children growing up and remaining within the worshipping community, and in mission terms towards those families, and others.

Preparation of the adults

I remember asking at my interview for my present job, in spring 2001, whether this church admitted children to communion prior to their confirmation. A very definite 'no' was the answer. I had in my previous post worked hard to deliver communion prior to confirmation to the children of that parish,[1] so had already rehearsed the delicate task of persuading adults to enable this practice to be a great step forward for the whole church.

The first step was to put this into the aims and objectives for the church, four years down the line, aiming for 2005. This was a church that had not had a mission statement with 'aims and objectives' so the whole thing was a bit of a jolt. People only tended to notice the immediate objectives, which included lowering the average age of the PCC. Some folk thought this meant I was going to murder them in their beds to open up vacancies, so by the time we'd assured them that this was not so, objectives for several years hence were not being taken in.

As the years went by, people started to read what I'd planned with the wardens and PCC for more than a year ahead, and so conversations began about the whole idea of allowing children to receive. Once people had got over the 'I didn't so why should they?' moment, they discovered what a good idea it was. So as 2005 drew closer, we scheduled some specific content for the PCC of that year,

- to discuss what communion means for each of us;
- to discuss baptism;
- to discuss confirmation.

This series of discussions was very helpful and took place in a very positive spirit.

The Diocesan Children's Officer had sent me a 'what to do' pack, and we continued to follow the instructions according to diocesan guidelines.

The next stage was to invite the Diocesan Children's Officer to convene a meeting for the whole parish. We also invited the incumbent of a parish where children had been receiving communion for several years, to share how it had affected the church. This meeting was well publicized:

- Everyone attending any service for the preceding month received a paper flier.
- A substantial article was placed in the parish magazine.
- It was advertised in the notices every week for the previous month.
- It was also advertised in our paper pew notices every week for the previous month.

The meeting was well attended, and our Children's Officer was very good. She took us through the history of this matter, and then the visiting incumbent told us about his church's experience. The dialogue was very healthy, and the vote at the end of the meeting well in favour.

The PCC voted at the next meeting 19–1 in favour. The next stage was to write to the bishop of the diocese asking for his permission to proceed. We had to send back the checklist from the guidelines including information about how we would prepare the children.

We had, along the way, purchased a couple of schemes. Off-the-shelf courses are great, but some tinkering is always needed to ensure you get what you really want, so once we received permission my curate and I sat down together and made up our own, to suit our children and our context.

The course itself[2]

A key factor with this enterprise is involving parents and carers with the children. Every child needs to be supported through this process, for the sake of both the child and the church, and it's also an excellent tool for mission and education back home! We therefore sent out a letter[3] to every child that we could think of who was even vaguely part of the church – the Sunday school, the choir, all the children who came to church-affiliated groups, etc. – inviting parents and children to a meeting after church one Sunday to discuss the possibility of their children receiving communion prior to confirmation. At that meeting, if the family was interested, they could pick up an application form, listing details of days and times and with a tear-off application form.[4]

In my present diocese, the youngest age for this scheme is 7.[5] Our first cohort of children included three 7-year-olds, and then rose to a couple of 13-year-olds, who would be confirmed later that year anyway. The course began with 16 children, dividing into two groups. We had hoped that the older children would group together, but they didn't, so both groups had the full age span. This was not ideal for the older ones, but they proved very helpful with the younger ones!

We allowed five sessions prior to the service, then another at the end, which became a real celebratory event for the whole church community.

The course was based around the structure of the communion or Eucharist service as follows:

- Week 1 Beginning and gathering.
- Week 2 Belonging, word, story.
- Week 3 Belonging in baptism; creed.
- Week 4 Story of the Last Supper (or Last Dinner). Remembering and sharing; Eucharistic prayer.
- Week 5 Sending out.

Essential kit

For each child we purchased:

- a school-type exercise book; the modern words of the Lord's Prayer were stuck in the inside cover;
- a pencil;
- a plastic 'book bag' to keep the book and pencil safe;
- lots of stickers.

Every week we came with a large themed outline drawing, which the children used as a frame for the week's prayer. These were stuck into the exercise books, along with the homework sheet.

The course took place in church. We set up a working area (tables, chairs, etc.) in one of our side aisles that is not usually needed for worship. We also had a large area of display boards ready to add to every week. On this we had a large outline of the church. The congregation were encouraged to look at this display as it logged our progress weekly. We had a flip-chart ready in the working area.

You will also need lots of glue sticks, colouring kits and various other craft supplies.

We always had at least two adults working behind the scenes with us.

On the Sunday before we began, all the children were listed in our weekly notice sheet. During the service, we brought them out and committed the whole church to praying for them as we travelled down through the weeks together.

Week 1: Exploring church

Set up

A treasure trail is laid around the church.[6] It ends at the altar. On the altar are the children's books, folders, pencils and pieces of paper (three per child, A4 size).

You need an outline drawing of your church almost as large as a page in the exercise books, one for each child. This is this week's prayer outline. You also need a note for each child of the homework for this week.

The session

1 Begin by welcoming the children.
2 Explain how the treasure hunt works; we give them the first clue, then when they arrive at that place the next clue is read out to the whole group, and so on. This keeps the smaller ones with the faster ones, and ensures that they all end together at the altar. Run through what each place you visit is for. What is the point of the pews? What is the lectern for? Why do we have an altar or table?
3 At the altar, you will find the books, etc. Hand out one of each per child, and lead them back to the working area.
4 The children now write their names on their pieces of paper, decorating them as they wish. (The finished names need to be laminated before the next session.)
5 Each child is given the prayer outline for the week, and sticks it into the book.
6 Discuss with the children what they would like as their prayer this week. (Try to keep it down to one sentence.) Write it on the flip-chart, and then the children write it into their prayer outline.

7 Each child is given seven stickers, and told that every day they need to pray the prayer with an adult, and then they stick a sticker for each day into their prayer outline.

8 Explain their homework: to bring in a photo or picture of themselves, ideally with other members of their family, to be included in the developing display in church. They can also use their books to record how life is for them, like a diary or a journal, but that's optional.

9 Ask the children to quietly go to any place in the church that they regard as particularly holy, where they will feel close to God. Spend a few moments in quiet, the children with their eyes closed and just focusing on that place. Say a clear 'Amen' so they know when the prayer time is finished, and then make sure they have their folders and everything inside that should be there before they go home.

Week 2: The Good Shepherd

Set up

This week's content is based around the Good Shepherd story from Godly Play.[7] Don't underestimate the amount of time it will take you to learn the session and to organize the materials; this is not a last-minute session! I used the chancel space to teach the lesson; you will need a suitable quiet space with enough room for the children to sit comfortably in a circle.

This week's prayer outline is that of a sheep; one per child.

Their names will have been laminated. You will need Blu Tack or similar to attach them to the display.

Art and craft materials need to be laid out at the working area.

The session

1 Welcome the children.

2 Talk through their homework. Look at the photographs, etc. and ask the helpers to attach them to the display. Let the children put their names up on the display.

3 Tell the story. Spend plenty of time wondering with them.
4 Ask them to do some work, reflecting on how the story made them feel. They return to the working area one at a time, and the helpers set up each child with materials. Once each child has finished his piece of work, let him place it in the display – if he wants to. Some may need to take theirs home to finish.
5 About seven minutes from the end, move on to this week's prayer. Write it on the flip-chart as they suggest what they would like to pray about this week. The children then write it into their outline. (We found it easiest if the helpers stuck these outlines into the children's books during the storytelling.)
6 Distribute this week's stickers and homework sheet. This week's homework is to bring in mementoes of their baptism.
7 Say the prayer together.

Week 3: Belonging – baptism

Set up

You need a small doll to baptize. Either use the font at the back of the church, or have a bowl of water. Bring a towel.

The prayer outline this week is of a candle; one per child.

You will also need a badge machine. Most dioceses or area youth offices will be able to lend you one of these. They can be the very devil to use – have a practice first!

Get your baptism register and have it ready to look at.

The session

1 Welcome the children.
2 Look at the mementoes of their baptism that they have brought. Some of them may remember being baptized; if so, encourage them to share. Some of the older ones may remember the baptisms of some of the youngest; encourage them to reminisce together.

3 Look in the baptism register for the names of the children who are present.

4 Take the children through a baptism, using the doll. Use the 'I wonder' formula that you used with Godly Play last week. Then chat about how adults are baptized – one of your helpers may like to experience this again!

5 Baptism is about joining the Church, belonging to the Church. Back at the work area, let each child design and make a badge about belonging to God and the Church. Ideally, make two copies of each; the second is added to the display.

6 Write this week's prayer. Distribute this week's stickers and homework sheet. Homework is to use the prayer at home.

Week 4: The Last Supper

Set up

This week's story is the Godly Play retelling of Jesus' Last Passover,[8] or Jesus and the Twelve.[9] Make sure you order or make the visual aids in plenty of time, so you can practise. I also used some pitta bread and very watery wine. Before the session, check with all parents and carers that it's OK to give their children bread and wine.

The prayer outline is of a chalice.

NB: The word 'supper' is not common parlance with children. You may need to explain this meal. Several of my children call this celebration 'Jesus' Last Dinner'.

The session

1 Welcome the children. If they have lots of energy, play a quick game of 'Where's this place?' using the correct names for parts of the building such as lectern, pulpit, Lady Chapel, etc.

2 Calm the children, and then lead them to the Godly Play space. I used the altar table in church, with the children standing in a circle around the table. You may prefer to be seated on the floor with them.

3 Tell them the story. If you are using real pitta and wine, hand it round at the appropriate point in the story.
4 Give the children time to wonder. Then go to the work area one at a time to do some work based on how the story made them feel. If they finish in time, they can add their work to the display. Some may need to finish at home.
5 Devise the prayer for this week. Say the prayer together.
6 Give out the stickers and homework sheet for this week. Homework is to use the prayer at home.

Week 5: Journeying together – 'Mission Possible!'

Set up

Each child will need an empty matchbox. You also need to prepare some work cards to illustrate the structure of the Eucharist, and how it's been reflected in the course.[10] You will need the vessels that are used to distribute communion, with the cloths that cover them.

The prayer outline this week is of a circle of people holding hands.

The session

1 Welcome the children. Give each one a matchbox, and challenge them to scour the church, finding as many things as they can to put in their matchbox.
2 Compare the contents. Explain that we sent them on a mission that sounded very hard (we have such a clean church) but they managed to find all these things. What do they think our mission is as Christians?
3 Using the work cards, work through the course, thinking about it in terms of where it has reflected the communion service:
   • gathering (treasure hunt, journey, beginning);
   • word (story, parable, learning);
   • creed (baptism, belief, peace, church as a family);

- Eucharistic prayer (remembering and sharing the Last Dinner);
- add this session – sending out (continuing the journey).

This leads on to the Eucharist liturgy. Put pictures with this list to reflect the liturgy. Use prayer pictures that have been photocopied and key words written in a large font to help illustrate this structure. Sequence and match the pictures and words to give a complete service structure, by putting pictures with key words. These then are in the order that they will occur during the liturgy.

4 Stress that it is important they need to keep going – to be a Christian we need to be sustained by Church and share together, etc.
5 To break up the words, play a quick game: run to where:
   - we sit in church (will vary – mainly nave);
   - we hear a story or the Bible or a sermon;
   - people are baptized – check understanding – belief in triune God.
6 Demonstrate how we greet each other in the middle of the service (shake hands).
7 Where is the Last Supper or Dinner re-enacted? Go to the altar rail and practise receiving communion, using the vessels they will use 'on the day'.
8 What happens at the end of the service? ('Go in peace to love and serve the Lord.')
9 Prayer for the week – ask the children how we serve God out in the world, and use that to build the prayer.

Week 6: The celebration (after the children have received)

Set up

Make sure the display is clearly visible. Organize whatever refreshments are going to be available. Have certificates ready.

The session

This session has no formal structure. It is important that all the church is invited, perhaps to share a meal together, and to talk with the children about why they wanted to receive, and how they feel now that they have achieved that aim. The children are all given a personalized certificate to mark the occasion.

It is also important to thank the members of the church for the support that they have extended to the children.

It is required that you note down the names of the children who receive, along with the date, in your parish confirmation book for future record.

Clearly, this course was devised for our church, at our time. Next time it will be different; use your initiative to fit a course for the group that you have – and enjoy!

Questions for discussion

1 How do you think your church would view allowing children to receive communion prior to confirmation?
2 Where do our attitudes towards receiving communion come from? Perhaps you could share your earliest memories and see if you can trace those very strong feelings that you have about this.
3 What benefit do you see for the children, and their families, through allowing children to receive in this way?
4 How would this affect your church?

Appendix 1

Shadrach, Meshach and Abednego and the amazing band

Who for?

Suitable for KS1 and KS2.

Aim

To encourage the children to be brave and stand up to those who would try to bully them into saying things that they don't believe in.

Preparation

Each group has a key word in the telling of the story. They need to be primed; the words are:

- horn
- pipe
- lyre
- trigon
- drum
- the whole band

and

- satraps
- prefects
- governors
- counsellors
- treasurers
- justices
- magistrates
- all the officials.

(The first group are musical instruments, the second administrative posts in ancient Babylon.)

You will need to use your initiative as to how you distribute the words.

You also need to put these two lists on to an OHP sheet or similar, so that when we get to that stage in the story, you can conduct the responses.

The session

You will need to explain what will happen. You are going to tell the story, but when you get to certain parts, you will bring in the children, whose words form a chorus within the story. They need to know when to come in, so you will point to their word on the OHP. Have at least one practice! It needs to run along as if one person were saying those words. Could be quite a challenge!

So, with the OHP in place, this is the story:

The story

King Nebuchadnezzar was the king of Babylon and the whole world, as he knew it. He was so important that he began to wonder if he might be a god. So, he made a golden statue. It was huge! It was so big he couldn't put it up in the city; he had to have it put up on the plains, so that all the people who lived in the city could see it, and the people who farmed outside the walls.

King Nebuchadnezzar called together all the people who helped him to rule Babylon; he called the

satraps,
prefects,
governors,
counsellors,
treasurers,
justices,
magistrates and
all the officials

and said to them, 'Tell the people this: when you hear the sound of the

horn,
pipe,

lyre,
trigon,
drum and
the whole band

everyone must bow down and worship my huge golden statue.'
So, the

satraps,
prefects,
governors,
counsellors,
treasurers,
justices,
magistrates and
all the officials

told all the people, 'This is what the King says: when you hear the sound
of the

horn,
pipe,
lyre,
trigon,
drum and
the whole band

playing, you must bow down and worship the huge golden statue of King
Nebuchadnezzar.'
The next day, there came the sound of the

horn,
pipe,
lyre,
trigon,
drum and
the whole band.

And all the people bowed down and worshipped the statue. Except for
three men. They knew that Nebuchadnezzar wasn't a god; they knew that
there was only one God, and they worshipped God, who made the heav-
ens and the earth. So they couldn't bow down and worship the huge gold-

en statue that King Nebuchadnezzar had made. They knew that they would get into awful trouble, but even when the people dragged them off to the King's court, they didn't change their minds. They knew it was wrong to worship a huge golden statue of the King, and they weren't going to do it.

To be continued . . .

Reflection

Ask the children to sit quietly and think about the story that they have just heard. What would they have done if they had been one of the men who didn't want to worship the statue? What do they have in their own lives that is so important to them that they never betray it, even if it meant disobeying such a strong rule?

To finish

Sing something upbeat and cheerful, like 'Give Me Joy in My Heart'.

Appendix 2
Letter of invitation

———•◆•———

January 2006

Dear Parents, Guardians and Children

You may have heard that St John's recently received permission from the Bishop for our children and young people to receive communion prior to confirmation, subject to them fulfilling a preparatory course. This letter is to invite you and your child (age guide approximately 7–14) to consider whether this is something you would like, and then to let you know the preparations that we are making in the next few months. Our intention is that the children will receive for the first time on Easter Sunday, 16 April, at the 10 a.m. service. From this Easter, this will take place annually, so if you or your child, having undertaken the course, do not feel this is the right year, there will be opportunity in the future.

This is something that families undertake together: there will be a couple of meetings for all the family to attend, five sessions for the children, and homework each week to be done with parents or guardians.

There will be two courses running in parallel: one on Mondays from 27 February, 4.30–5.15 p.m., and one on Thursdays from 2 March, 5–5.45 p.m. (just before choir practice), with a final session after church on 30 April for all of us. You can choose the day you prefer, and should a child be ill or unable to attend one meeting, theoretically they could attend the 'other' session that week.

Everyone interested (adults and children) needs to attend a meeting in the church hall at 11.30 on Sunday 29 January.

All children must have been baptized. If your child has not been baptized and would like to receive communion, we can arrange for baptism to take place in due course.

Please could you return the slip below to me at the Vicarage to give us an idea of numbers.

With my best wishes

We will be attending the meeting on 29 January.

Name of child ....

Date of birth ....

Signed ....Parent/Guardian

Telephone ....

E-mail ....

Appendix 3
Application form

Children and communion: a preparation course

Monday course: 4.30–5.15 in the church
February 27
March 6 Painting – bring protective clothing
      13 Please bring baptism mementoes
      20 Painting – bring protective clothing
      27
April 16 Easter Day
April 30 All-age communion at 10 a.m. followed by a celebratory brunch. Please bring your completed diaries.

My child will be attending the Monday course (Ronni)

Name of child ....

Date of birth ....

Address ....

Tel. ....

E-mail ....

Signed ....Parent/Guardian

Appendix 4
Treasure trail

Where might Mary be?	(Lady Chapel)
Where we make babies wet	(Font)
A big book is found here!	(Lectern)
Where we give out the books	(Entrance way)
Where most people sit	(Pews)
The vicar's name is here	(List of ministers)
This can make lots of noise!	(Organ)
This is where people sing	(Choir stalls)
Ronni (vicar) sits here	(Clergy stall)
Up the steps to say the words	(Pulpit)
Bread and wine are found here	(Altar)

Appendix 5
Work cards

Gathering (treasure hunt, journey, beginning)
Word (story, parable, learning)
Creed (baptism, belief, peace, church as a family)
Eucharistic prayer (remembering and sharing the Last Dinner)
Add this session – sending out (continuing the journey)

Notes

1 Introduction

1 1 Corinthians 13.11.

2 This is not so for some people with learning difficulties, who may not move out of their childish thinking.

3 Jerome Berryman (1991), *Godly Play*.

4 D. Hay and R. Nye (1998), *The Spirit of the Child*.

5 I use 'sin' as an example as it seems to me that most people outside the Church and those who are regarded as 'fringe members' may have a very limited understanding of what the word means. It is not often heard in the vernacular any longer in this country, and even within the Church understanding of this concept is sometimes very limited.

6 It is, of course, possible to talk about God without being spiritual. Many discussions at university for those reading for a degree in theology, philosophy or other similar disciplines will debate God for hours, in a purely academic way. We each have our own unique concept of God, no matter the type of background from which we come, much as I have a concept of 'Disneyland' without having experienced the reality.

7 This is very noticeable when interviewers tackle people such as the Archbishop of Canterbury; they often relate to their spirituality with a very childlike understanding, which communicates as peculiarly out of step with their clearly well-advanced adult intellectual thinking.

8 William Wordsworth, 'Intimations of Immortality from Recollections of Early Childhood'.

9 J. Loder (1989), *The Transforming Moment*.

10 See Hay and Nye for more detail.

3 Personality

1 Toddler training books recommend the following: when the child cries, wait for five minutes, then go in and stroke her, but do not

lift her from the bed or cot. Say a few calming words, then leave the room. Keep repeating every five minutes. We had sleepless nights for two years, tried this and it worked the first night, after 15 minutes and three visits. It's very, very hard, so parents are usually quite desperate by the time they do it, and this will give them the will-power to manage the strategy.

2 There are, of course, more stages in Erikson's scheme – do look at them if this has caught your interest.

4 Social development

1 Especially 'Stairway to Heaven' from Led Zep 4.
2 William Golding (1954), *Lord of the Flies*, London, Faber.
3 John Harding (2006), *One Big Damn Puzzler*, London, Black Swan.
4 H.R. Schaffer (1984), *The Child's Entry into a Social World*.
5 L.A. Kirkpatrick and P.R. Shaver (1992), 'Attachment Theory and Religion'.

5 Faith, and how it grows

1 Fowler divides our faith life into six distinct stages. For more detail, see James Fowler (1995), *Stages of Faith*.
2 Fowler's research began with interviews with children who were 4 years old. Comments regarding younger children are deduced from cognitive development theory and observation.
3 See Ana-Maria Rizzuto (1979), *The Birth of the Living God*.
4 There are three more stages of faith, but they do not fall within the scope of this book. If you would like to read more about them and reflect on what Fowler has to say, most ministers have some of his work on their bookshelves, and there may be a local minister who has studied Fowler in depth who can help. I recommend General Synod Board of Education (1991), *How Faith Grows*.
5 See John Westerhoff (2000), *Will Our Children Have Faith?*
6 There are two more styles of faith in Westerhoff's scheme. As with the later stages of Fowler's scheme of faith development, they fall outside the remit of this book, but you can read about them in Westerhoff's writing.

6 An overview

1 At the time of writing, the Christian Unions in many universities have become even more fundamental than they were in my own student days. The type of faith that they seem to espouse is authoritarian and closed – very much Fowler's Stage 3. This means there is a danger that young people of faith who are attending to the questions and doubts of Stage 4 are not able to find support in such a group, and may give up their Christianity as a response.
2 I have such a group in my present church. We meet once a month and talk about things which concern them, and I encourage them to bring ideas to this meeting to pass on to the adult church meetings. It has been very good to hear their ideas, which are often very much in line with the adult thinking, and to value these young people as real members of the church, not just 'the church in waiting'.

7 Godly Play

1 The fact that many ministers feel that they are 'not good with children' reinforces this way of sidelining children from the main body of the church during worship, and so from the day-to-day life of most of the worshippers.
2 See Appendix 1 for a script of how to turn this story into an interactive telling. Also see <www.assemblies.org>, where it appears as a school assembly.
3 See J. Berryman (1995), *Teaching Godly Play*.
4 See the script for 'The Good Shepherd' in S. Stewart and J. Berryman (1989), *Young Children and Worship*, pp. 85ff.
5 Ronni Lamont (2004), 'A comparison of the effect of storytelling on the spirituality of children aged 9 and 10', MA (Pastoral Theology) dissertation, Anglia Polytechnic University (now Anglia Ruskin University).
6 Ronni Lamont, as above.
7 Ronni Lamont, as above.
8 Ronni Lamont, as above.

8 Children thinking about God

1 My thanks go to Peter Wilson and the children of Old Bexley (C. of E.) Primary School, and to Tony Linnett and the children of Hurst Primary School, for their input.

2 The turning away from fairy stories that has taken place over the last 30 years or so reflects this trend; people say that they don't want to expose their children to such violent and grisly stories, without realizing that one function of the grisly fairy story is to help children rehearse scenarios in their heads before they come across them in reality, and that these stories are actually very moral. For possibly the best book dealing with this, see Bruno Bettelheim (1976/1991), *The Uses of Enchantment*.

3 For out-of-print books I recommend <www.alibris.com>, an American site that sells second-hand and out-of-print books, which has never let me down. It's also very cheap!

4 For young children, *Badger's Parting Gifts* by Susan Varley (London, Picture Lions, 1994) is a delightful exploration of death. For older children, *Waterbugs and Dragonflies* by Doris Stickney (London, Continuum, 2002) is very helpful.

5 See <www.assemblies.org>, a site run by SPCK, for examples of assemblies, with prayer and reflection for children of this age.

6 Defining God by saying what God is not is part of the apophatic tradition.

7 Is this a flashback to watching *Tellytubbies* (BBC/Wood Productions) when smaller, where the sun had a laughing cherubic toddler face superimposed?

8 This classic reasoning for God's existence is called the ontological argument.

9 I use the version in *The Complete Guide to Godly Play* by Jerome Berryman, vol. 3, or see <www.godlyplay.org>.

10 From *The Complete Guide to Godly Play*.

9 The way forward

1 What is now called an NQT year.

2 Adults access the service in different ways. *The Dynamics of Religion* by Bruce Reed (1978) gives a fascinating insight into what's going on in people's heads during a service.

3 If you take out the pews, enjoy the chairs – move them around! Don't pretend you're moving on towards more flexible styles of worship if you're not! What a waste of good money! Build an extension for the Sunday school instead.

4 At my present church, this became a group for parents of younger children, nearly all of whom are or have been Sunday school teachers. We now have two meetings, one to plan the curriculum and events, and another for fellowship needs. We meet in the local deli for a late breakfast . . .

5 Insert your number here!

10 A sharing of 'good practice'

1 We had not been successful. The parish was a team, including an ecumenical church (Anglican/RC/Baptist). If a parish is to proceed with communion prior to confirmation, all the churches in the team must go forward together. Unfortunately the Baptist element was not able to agree to this, so all of the churches in the team were prevented from going down this path. Yes, it was very frustrating!

2 I'm very grateful to my curate, Revd Juliet Donnelly, for her input to this course, which we devised together.

3 See Appendix 2.

4 See Appendix 3.

5 This is the age recommended by General Synod. I have to admit to finding it fairly arbitrary; it's very small children who desperately put up their hands for communion at the rail. By the time they reach 7, they've learned that they won't get any. We agreed to two rising 7s in this cohort as both had older siblings and clearly wanted to be included. The decision was reached by balancing how much damage excluding these children would cause, in discussion with parents and carers. As much of the debate about giving children communion at this age is to do with inclusion, it was felt we would be doing more damage by saying no to these youngsters. They were all excellent students, and received with great joy and respect.

6 See Appendix 4.

7 Materials for Godly Play sessions can be bought from St Michael's Community Trust, <www.bowthorpecommtrust@

lineone.net>, 01603 746106. They take about six weeks to arrive. Or you can find a keen craftsperson to make these visual aids. Patterns are included in the books. The story is found in Stewart and Berryman's *Young Children and Worship*, pp. 85ff., or in Berryman's *The Complete Guide to Godly Play*, vol. 3.

8 This is found in Stewart and Berryman, pp. 189ff.
9 From Berryman, *The Complete Guide to Godly Play*, vol. 4, pp. 81ff.
10 See Appendix 5.

Bibliography

Axline, V., *Dibs in Search of Self*, Penguin, London, Ballantine, 1990

Bee, H. and Boyd, D., *The Developing Child*, London, Allyn and Bacon, 2006

Berryman, J., *Godly Play*, Minneapolis, Augsburg Fortress, 1991

Berryman, J., *Teaching Godly Play*, Nashville, Abingdon, 1995

Berryman, J., *The Complete Guide to Godly Play*, vols 3 and 4, New York, Living the Good News, 2002 (or see <www.godlyplay. org>)

Best, E., *Mark: The Gospel as Story*, Edinburgh, T&T Clark, 1983

Bettelheim, B., *The Uses of Enchantment*, London, Penguin, 1976/1991

Cavaletti, S., *The Religious Potential of the Child*, New York, Paulist Press, 1979

Coggin, J.R. and Houlden, J.L., *A Dictionary of Biblical Interpretation*, London/Philadelphia, SCM/TPI, 1990

Coles, R., *The Spiritual Life of Children*, Boston, Houghton Mifflin, 1990

Copsey, K., *From the Ground Up*, Oxford, Barnabas, 2005

Erikson, E., *Childhood and Society*, London, Vintage, 1995

Fowler, J., *Faith Development and Pastoral Care*, Philadelphia, Fortress Press, 1987

Fowler, J., *Stages of Faith*, San Francisco, Harper, 1995

Fowler, J., Nipkow, K. and Schweitzer, F., *Stages of Faith and Religious Development*, London, SCM Press, 1991

General Synod Board of Education, *Children in the Way*, London, NS/CHP, 1988

General Synod Board of Education, *All God's Children?*, London, NS/CHP, 1991

General Synod Board of Education, *How Faith Grows*, London, NS/CHP, 1991

Goldingay, J., *After Eating the Apricot*, Cumbria, Solway, 1996

Hay, D., *Something There*, London, DLT, 2006

Hay, D. and Nye, R., *The Spirit of the Child*, London, Fount, 1998

Hopewell, J.F., *Congregation: Stories and Structures*, Minneapolis, Augsburg Fortress, 1987

Kirkpatrick, L.A. and Shaver, P.R., 'Attachment Theory and Religion: Childhood Attachments, Religious Beliefs and Conversion', *Journal for the Scientific Study of Religion*, 29, 3: 315–34, 1992.

Lamont, R., 'A Comparison of the Effect of Storytelling on the Spirituality of Children aged 9 and 10', MA (Pastoral Theology) dissertation, Anglia Polytechnic University (now Anglia Ruskin University), 2004

Loder, J., *The Transforming Moment*, Colorado Springs, Helmers and Howard, 1989

Pollerman, S., *Stories, Stories Everywhere*, Oxford, Barnabas, 2001

Reed, B., *The Dynamics of Religion*, London, DLT, 1978

Rizzuto, A.-M., *The Birth of the Living God*, University of Chicago Press, 1979

Schaffer, H.R., *The Child's Entry into a Social World*, London, Academic Press, 1984

Slee, N., 'Parable Teaching: Exploring New Worlds', *British Journal of Religious Education*, 5, 1983

Stewart, S. and Berryman, J., *Young Children and Worship*, Louisville, Westminster John Knox Press, 1989

Tamminem, K., *Religious Development in Childhood and Youth*, Helsinki, Suomalainen Tiedeakatemia, 1991

Walker, A., *Telling the Story*, London, SPCK, 1996

Watts, F., Nye, R. and Savage, S., *Psychology for Christian Ministry*, London, Routledge, 2002

Westerhoff, J., *Will Our Children Have Faith?*, Harrisburg, Penn., Morehouse Publishing, 2000

Withers, M., *Mission-Shaped Children*, London, Church House Publishing, 2006

Wolff Pritchard, G., *Offering the Gospel to Children*, Cambridge, Mass., Cowley Publications, 1992

Wood, D., *How Children Think and Learn*, Oxford, Blackwell, 1998

Index